NOW! A NEW METHOD OF LEARNING THE THRILLING SPORT OF JUDO!! YOU DO NOT HAVE TO MAKE JUDO A "WAY OF LIFE" TO ENJOY ITS MANY BENEFITS.

All the techniques needed to progress from beginner to Black Belt are taught in this book; in addition, there is a section of basic self-defense which can be learned by ANYBODY.

Bruce Tegner faithfully follows the original ideas of the founder of Judo, Dr. Jigaro Kano, adapting those ideas to the needs of twentieth-century people.

Also by Bruce Tegner

COMPLETE BOOK OF KARATE
COMPLETE BOOK OF JUKADO SELF-DEFENCE
BRUCE TEGNER METHOD OF SELF–DEFENCE
BRUCE TEGNER'S COMPLETE BOOK OF AIKIDO
AND HOLDS AND LOCKS

and published by Corgi Books

BRUCE TEGNER

COMPLETE BOOK OF JUDO

CORGI BOOKS
A DIVISION OF TRANSWORLD PUBLISHERS LTD

DEDICATION:

This book is dedicated to
those who question, doubt and
deny; they bring us to truth.

COMPLETE BOOK OF JUDO

A CORGI BOOK 552 07917 0

First publication in Great Britain

PRINTING HISTORY
Corgi Edition published 1968
Corgi Edition reprinted 1970
Corgi Edition reprinted 1972
Corgi Edition reprinted twice 1974

The author wishes to thank
Richard Windishar, Elise Simmons,
Robert Simmons, Don Phillips and
Gordon White for assisting him in
demonstrating the techniques in photos.

Grateful acknowledgment it made to
Helen Phillips, Don Phillips, Mike Hazy and
Cynthia Blessing for help in preparation
of this manuscript.

*This manuscript was prepared under the
supervision of Alice McGrath.*

This book is set in Times New Roman

Corgi Books are published by Transworld Publishers Ltd,
Cavendish House, 57–59 Uxbridge Road, Ealing, London W5

Printed Offset in Great Britain by
Fletcher & Son Ltd, Norwich

Note: The Australian price appearing on the back cover
is the recommended retail price.

CONTENTS

INTRODUCTION AND PRE-INSTRUCTION

IS JUDO A WAY OF LIFE? / 11

COLORED BELT RANKS / 14

THE BLACK BELT / 16

IS SPORT JUDO FOR SELF-DEFENSE? / 16

JAPANESE VOCABULARY / 16

JUDO UNIFORM / 17

KI-YA (SUPERPOWER) / 18

THE FALLS OF JUDO, A NEW APPROACH / 18

HOW TO PRACTICE / 19

SAFETY RULES FOR JUDO PRACTICE / 20

EXERCISES / 24

PRACTICE AND CONTEST STANCES / 36

BODY MECHANICS / 36

BALANCES / 37

CANTING / 40

TILTING / 41

COMBINATION CANTING, TILTING AND LIFTING / 41

BODY REACTION / 43

MUSCLE REACTION / 43

USING OPPONENT'S STRENGTH / 45

FOLLOWTHROUGH ARM WORK / 45

SHADOW THROWING / 46

FOOTWORK / 49

PIVOTS / 50

SLOW-MOTION ANALYSIS OF THROWS / 54

PROCEDURE FOR TESTS—FORMAL THROWING
  FOR BELT DEGREES / 56

HONORARY, FORM, WOMEN'S AND JUNIOR DEGREES / 57

INDIVIDUAL STYLE OF JUDO PLAY / 57

PART TWO

FALLS, THROWS, FREE-STYLE PRACTICE, AND FORMAL DEMONSTRATIONS FOR BELT DEGREES

GREEN BELT REQUIREMENTS AND TRAINING / 58

  GREEN BELT FALLS / 60

  GREEN BELT THROWS / 69

     HIP THROW / 69
     NECK THROW / 72
     OVER-SHOULDER THROW / 72
     ONE-ARM OVER-SHOULDER THROW / 72
     KICKBACK THROW / 74
     STRAIGHT FOOT THROW / 76
     LATERAL DASH THROW / 78
     CIRCLE THROW / 79
   FREE-STYLE EXERCISE / 80
   ADDITIONAL TRAINING:
     SALUTATION BOW AND THE COURTESY THROW / 81
     TIPS FOR TALL MEN / 82
     TIPS FOR SHORT MEN / 82
     COUNTERS AGAINST STIFF-ARMING / 84
     HOW TO BLOCK THROWS / 88
     TACTICAL USE OF THROWS FOR FREE-STYLE PRACTICE AND
       CONTEST / 90
        PRACTICE AND CONTEST / 90
THIRD-DEGREE BROWN BELT REQUIREMENTS / 96
   THIRD BROWN BELT FALLS / 97
   THIRD BROWN BELT THROWS / 103
     SWEEPING FOOT THROW / 103
     KNEECAP THROW / 104
     SWEEPING LOIN THROW / 105
     UPPER INNERCUT THROW / 107
     SPRING FOOT THROW / 107
     INNERCUT THROW / 108
   COMBINATION THROWS / 109
   MAT TECHNIQUES:
     HOLDING / 112
   ADDITIONAL TRAINING:
     MAT WORK, BASIC PROCEDURES / 118
     HOW TO EVADE GROUND WORK IF YOU ARE THROWN / 121
     HOW TO BREAK HOLDS / 122
     CONTEST WORK:
       PREPARATION FOR CONTEST / 131
       RULES OF CONTEST / 131
       TYPES OF CONTEST / 134
       USE OF PSYCHOLOGY IN CONTEST / 135
SECOND-DEGREE BROWN BELT REQUIREMENTS / 135
   SECOND BROWN BELT THROWS / 136
     LIFTING SWEEPING FOOT THROW / 136
     INSIDE SWEEPING FOOT THROW / 137
     BACK SWEEPING FOOT THROW / 138
     OUTERCUT THROW / 138
     PULLING-DOWN STRAIGHT FOOT THROW / 138
     SIDE SWEEPING FOOT THROW / 140
   COMBINATION THROWS / 140

MAT TECHNIQUES:
  HOLDING / 144
  CHOKES / 145
  ARM LOCKS / 146
ADDITIONAL TRAINING:
  RELEASES FROM CHOKES AND LOCKS / 149
FIRST-DEGREE BROWN BELT REQUIREMENTS / 150
  FIRST BROWN BELT THROWS / 150
    REAR HIP THROW / 150
    REVERSE HIP THROW / 151
    BINDING THROW / 152
    SHOULDERING THROW / 152
    CRAB CLAW THROW / 154
    INSIDE LATERAL DASH THROW / 154
  COMBINATION THROWS / 154
  MAT TECHNIQUES:
    CHOKES / 158
    ARM LOCKS AND ANKLE LOCK / 159
BLACK BELT REQUIREMENTS / 161
  FORMAL THROWING: CEREMONY AND PROCEDURE / 162
  TRADITIONAL PRELIMINARY MOVEMENTS / 162
  FIRST BLACK BELT THROWS / 161
    PULLING DOWN THROW / 164
    ONE-ARM OVER-SHOULDER THROW / 165
    SHOULDERING THROW / 166
    HIP THROW / 166
    SWEEPING LOIN THROW / 168
    LEVERING ARM HIP THROW / 168
    SIDE SWEEPING FOOT THROW / 168
    SIFTING SWEEPING FOOT THROW / 170
    UPPER INNERCUT THROW / 170
    CIRCLE THROW / 170
    BACK BODY SACRIFICE THROW / 172
    INSIDE LATERAL DASH THROW / 172
    REAR SWEEPING FOOT AND TAKEDOWN THROW / 172
    SIDE BODY SACRIFICE THROW / 174
    ANKLE LATERAL DASH THROW / 174
  SYSTEM OF RESUSCITATION:
    FIRST AID; RESPONSIBILITY, MORAL AND LEGAL / 176
    REVIVAL FROM UNCONSCIOUSNESS / 176

PART THREE

FORMAL THROWS FOR BELT DEGREES—OLD STYLE

INTRODUCTION TO FORM DEGREES / 180
REQUIREMENTS FOR DEGREES / 181

MOVEMENTS FOR CEREMONIAL PROCEDURES / 181
SECOND-DEGREE BROWN BELT REQUIREMENTS FORM DEGREE / 182
  MAT-WORK FORMS:
    FIRST SET—HOLDS / 182
    SECOND SET—CHOKES / 184
    THIRD SET—LOCKS / 188
FIRST-DEGREE BROWN BELT REQUIREMENTS FORM DEGREE / 190
  COUNTERTHROW FORMS / 190
FIRST-DEGREE BLACK BELT REQUIREMENTS FORM DEGREE / 196
  OLD-STYLE SELF-DEFENSE FORMS / 197
    FIRST SET—SEATED ATTACKS / 198
    SECOND SET—STANDING ATTACKS / 204

PART FOUR

SELF-DEFENSE AND SPORT FORMS—NEW STYLE

TIMES HAVE CHANGED! / 214
SELF-DEFENSE FORMS / 214
SPORT FORMS / 220

PART FIVE

BASIC SELF-DEFENSE

INTRODUCTION / 228
HOW TO KICK: FIVE BEST FOOT BLOWS / 230
HOW TO STRIKE: FIVE BEST HAND BLOWS / 230
NERVE CENTERS AND PRESSURE POINTS / 232
WHERE TO STRIKE:
  NONVIOLENT ATTACKS / 232
    LOW TARGET AREAS / 234
    REAR TARGET AREAS / 234
ANNOYING SITUATIONS / 236
FRONT GRAB—ANNOYING AND SERIOUS / 236
WRIST GRAB DEFENSES / 236
FRONT CHOKE DEFENSES / 238
FIRST FIGHTING DEFENSES / 238
THREATENED ATTACK / 242
CLUB ATTACKS / 242
BACK GRABS / 244
BACK CHOKE / 246
HAIR GRAB / 247
SURPRISE BACK ATTACK / 248
KICK DEFENSES / 248
THREATENED KNIFE ATTACK / 250
KNIFE ATTACK / 252
GANG ATTACKS / 254

ABOUT BRUCE TEGNER

Bruce Tegner is regarded as the most experienced instructor in America in the field of Oriental fighting arts for sports and self-defense.

He was, literally, born to Judo. Both his parents were Black Belt holders and professional instructors in the Judo—Jiu-Jitsu arts. By a fascinating coincidence, his birthdate is the same as that of Dr. Jigaro Kano, the Founder of Judo—October 28. His nursery was a miniature Judo practice hall and his formal training began when he was two years old! Until he was eight, his mother and his father taught him the fundamentals of Judo. After that, he was trained by high-ranking Oriental and European masters. His training covered many aspects of the various types of unarmed fighting as well as stick and sword fighting. In a field where specialization was (and still is) the tradition, Mr. Tegner's background is unusual.

At 15, when most youngsters are just beginning their training, Bruce Tegner was already a professional instructor; his natural ability and trained skill made him an outstanding teacher even then.

Until he was 17, Mr. Tegner was learning, teaching and competing in tournament. He won his Second Black Belt contest and in 1949 he became the California State Judo Champion. He was then the youngest Second-Degree Black Belt on record in the United States.

Because training for contest is not compatible with teaching, he gave up competition after this tournament and has since devoted his entire time and energy to teaching and research.

In the U.S. Armed Forces, Bruce Tegner served as instructor to teachers of weaponless combat and he was the coach for a number of special services Sport Judo teams.

Although Bruce Tegner was trained in the old method, he began to introduce innovations as soon as he began to teach. He realized that the old methods were outdated, even though it was generally thought that the traditional style of teaching was the only "authentic" way. During his service with the armed forces, he began the long-range application of his new style of teaching and was phenomenally successful. In that situation it was necessary to teach as much as possible to as many people as possible in the shortest time possible; the Bruce Tegner Method met the test!

After leaving the service, Mr. Tegner continued to improve his teaching methods with the aim of perfecting a system which would be most useful to most people, taking into consideration differences in individual goal, purpose and ability.

Since 1952, Bruce Tegner has had his own school in Hollywood where he has taught thousands of men, women and children.

He has devised a special course of instruction which is used by law-enforcement agencies all over the world and by police science departments in colleges throughout the United States. He has been employed by the U.S. government to train border-patrol personnel and Treasury agents. Movies and TV studios frequently call on him for expert technical advice, instruction of actors and invention of spectacular fight scenes.

With the appearance of this title, he will have 18 published books in print with additional titles in preparation.

IS JUDO A WAY OF LIFE?

There is a popular misconception which implies that Judo must be approached with an almost religious reverence. It is said that Judo is not merely a physical activity; it is a Way of Life. If you ask a modern proponent of the Way of Life notion what he means by the phrase, two related ideas develop: 1. That you must devote your entire life to the study of Judo, making it your central activity; 2. That through the serious study of Judo you will mysteriously and automatically become a more spiritual, highly moral person. Neither of these explanations has validity. Before we examine the attitudes of Judo's founder, Dr. Jigoro Kano, let us make a very brief survey of Judo history.

The origin and history of most of the Oriental unarmed arts cannot be reconstructed. Beginning thousands of years ago in China, practiced in secret and spreading throughout the Orient in different forms, no written records of their development were kept. Though theories differ, there seems to be general agreement that Chinese monks first used techniques of weaponless fighting to protect themselves from bandits. It is not known which type of unarmed technique was discovered first, but it is clear that specialization was the custom. In one area, the art of throwing would be known; in another area the art of choking was developed; in still another part of the country, the art of striking with the hands and feet would be learned; and elsewhere it would be the art of bending or twisting the joints. Combinations of different forms of fighting were unknown. Within these special forms of fighting there were subdivisions based on *subtle* differences. As the knowledge of weaponless fighting spread through the Orient, coming last to Japan, the subdivisions multiplied as did the names by which the arts were known. For the sake of simplicity, the ancient forms of fighting are called Jitsu—Wa Jitsu, Tai Jitsu, Go-Shin Jitsu, Ai-Jitsu, and many, many others. We would also call Yawara and ancient Karate types of Jitsus.

During most of the time that weaponless fighting was developing in the Orient, its use was illegal and practice was done in secret. Because of the secrecy and illegality, the Oriental weaponless fighting arts were the subject of many tales of fantasy and nonsense—some of which persist today.

In the middle of the 1860's, Dr. Jigoro Kano, a Japanese college professor (later a member of the House of Peers and a college president), began a systematic study of the many forms of Jitsu then practiced in Japan. Although the practice of weaponless fighting was no longer illegal, among students of the art there remained a cultish, fanatical attitude—a holdover from feudal habit.

Dr. Kano found that the men who knew one particular form of unarmed fighting had no knowledge or appreciation of any other form. They defended their own style of work as much out of ignorance of other techniques as they did from a conviction that it was effective. There was no thought of eliminating outdated techniques and no interest in improving the method of teaching. Far from trying to popularize the study of weaponless fighting, the teachers thought of themselves as an elite group and so encouraged the cult of mystery and purposely made learning difficult for the student. Among the fractionated, cultist groups, Dr. Kano found that there was no theory or understanding of work. It was a "trick" or a "secret" passed on from teacher to pupil.

Dr. Kano spent many years in the study of the ancient fighting arts, evaluating, comparing, and practicing. Finally, in 1882 he synthesized what he had learned and thus created a new art which was known as Judo. Literally, Judo means "the gentle way." If it could be interpreted as "the *easier* way," it would be more understandable, for Dr. Kano was explaining that the most efficient way *of doing anything* is "the gentle way." He was suggesting that the use of intellect, not merely the use of muscle, would be a "gentling" of the way of meeting the world and its practical problems. It was this idea which Dr. Kano intended should be the basis of a "Way of Life."

The following is a quotation from Dr. Kano: "*. . . there should be one all-pervading principle governing the whole field, and that principle should be the highest or most efficient use of mental as well as physical energy directed to the accomplishment of a certain definite purpose or aim. Once the real import of this principle is understood, it may be applied to all phases of life and activity, thereby enabling one to lead the highest and most rational life.*"

So, far from being a mystical means of getting plugged into a Higher Truth, Dr. Kano meant the "way" as a guide to rational and reasonable conduct in every phase of life. Dr. Kano felt that training to meet a Judo opponent in a "gentler way," and realizing its efficiency, would train the student to "meet all of life" in a gentler way, without force.

The only extravagance in Dr. Kano's concept is his contention that this lesson would be learned automatically. He failed to distinguish between the possibility that a student would learn the lesson and the possibility that a student would learn Judo very well without learning the lesson. To quote from La Rochefoucauld: ". . . there are no experiences so disastrous that thoughtful men cannot derive some profit from them nor so happy that the thoughtless cannot use them to their harm." In order to learn the useful lessons of Judo and apply them to the conduct of your life, you must *want* to understand and apply them.

Dr. Kano felt that the practice of the formal movements of Judo— "a combination of movements of limbs, neck and body in such a way that their combination may result in the harmonious development of the body as well as the inculcation of a high moral ideal"—led to *automatic* moral uplift. He would have had to revise his notion of the automatic spiritual values of calisthenics had he seen the youth of Germany and Japan engaged in their exercises just before and during the Second World War.

Modern proponents of Judo as a Way of Life make a mistake when they assume that "devotion to the art," to use their phrase, is the *only* way to a physical and mental harmony which could lead to a better, more useful, more reasonable and more pleasureable life. Dr. Kano's concept of most efficient use of mental and physical energy for the accomplishment of a definite purpose is not the exclusive property of Judo or Judo players. To make such a claim is not in the interest of promoting Judo play—tennis players use it, swimmers know it, fencers learn it—we could go on and on. Judo is wonderful, but it is not The Only Way. If it were, all Judo players would be, in Dr. Kano's words, "earnest, sincere, thoughtful, cautious and deliberate in all dealings, [would have] a high degree of mental composure [and would have developed] to a high degree the exercise of the power of imagination, of reasoning and of judgment applied at all times to the activities of daily life." As this is not so, we are allowed to question the "Way of Life" benefits of Judo practice.

To propose Judo as a Way of Life is to limit its acceptance. However, we can strongly recommend the practice of Judo on the basis of demonstrable benefits which have usefulness in modern life; Judo is splendid exercise and, unlike many exercises, it is great fun to do. Judo is marvelous for mind-body coordination; it is a participation rather than a spectator activity; and it is possible, if you have the desire, to improve all other activities of your life if you will apply what you have learned in Judo practice.

In this mechanized American era, we desperately need to encourage great numbers of people to participate in physical activity. We are a nation of watchers, and we cannot continue this trend without impoverishing our mental and physical health. (Lack of exercise, it has been proven, affects mental activity too.) The idea of Judo, it seems to me, is particularly appropriate for Americans. It can be played by men, women and children; it can be played for easy, friendly contest or for big tournament; it can be practiced for exercise. Judo need not be thought of as a Way of Life, but it can be a marvelous way to enrich your life.

And what about the notion that Judo, to be studied seriously, must be the central activity of your life? This is sheer nonsense. If the only people allowed to practice Judo were those who had the time and inclination to make it the most important activity of their lives, we would have only a tiny handful of Judo players in the entire country. Obviously, the amount of time you spend at Judo must be determined by many factors—the responsibility you have to your school work, your job, your family, and the like. The purpose for which you are studying Judo will also determine the amount of time you will want and need to spend at it: if your aim is to engage in an enjoyable, healthful few hours of exercise each week, Judo is not going to be the central activity of your life; if you want to become a champion Judo tournament player then it certainly will have to be the primary activity. And there are degrees of involvement between these two extremes; yours is the job of deciding the amount and degree of your commitment. There is nothing in Dr. Kano's presentation of Judo to indicate otherwise.

This book follows Dr. Kano's original concept: the division of Judo into its sport and self-defense aspects. Further, it follows Dr. Kano's concept of the importance of evaluation and change. Dr. Kano made drastic changes in the forms of the ancient Jitsus to suit the needs of his time; the acceptance of change is inherent in his method. Everything about his approach encourages us to make changes as they are required. Dr. Kano gave leadership with original and inventive thinking, but his followers have institutionalized his originality and want to make further originality a heresy.

By encouraging players of moderate ability, by encouraging players who would not accept Judo as a Way or Life, by encouraging Judo play in the same way we encourage weekly bowling, tennis and swimming, I hope that this book will help to gain for Judo in America that popularity which it deserves.

COLORED BELT RANKS

In their orginal forms, the unarmed fighting arts had no ranks, degrees, uniforms or belts.

Awarding belts for proficiency is a relatively new procedure. Sport Judo belts were first given approximately 85 years ago. Karate belts are less than 30 years old! Now, belt ranks are given in many other forms of the martial arts.

One rule is absolute: An individual may *not* grade himself in belt rank. No matter how hard he has studied, nor how sincere he is in his practice of the arts, no individual is capable of determining his own proficiency. That judgment must be made by someone who is in a position to evaluate the individual in terms of comparison. Proficiency has no meaning unless it is in relationship to the proficiency of other students.

Hopefully, there will come a time in Judo when the various styles, systems and organizations of the sport will be more generous in their recognition of belts earned in other styles and systems. At the present time, the various styles, schools and teachers do not usually "recognize" belts which are earned in a different style or school. Students should not be concerned about "official" or "authentic" belt gradings. If a belt is issued by a person competent to judge rank level, that belt is honestly earned, no matter in what system.

THE COLORS

Just as there are many different styles of training in Judo, there are many different schemes for belt ranking. In Japan the prevailing scheme is White Belt to designate novice, Brown Belt to show intermediate and Black Belt for advanced degrees. In much of the United States, there is the same system, with the addition of Green Belt to designate a rank between the beginner and intermediate degrees. Europe, which is more independent of Japan, has a better system of belting: allotting a belt color to each grade in the ranks. In the white-brown-black scheme there is no distinction (in belt) between the beginner on his first day of training and the man who will tomorrow go into competition for Brown Belt. There is a great deal of difference in ability and it should logically be marked, as it is by the Europeans.

The difference between White Belt and Brown Belt might be only a year. The length of time and training which separates the new Brown Belt from the first Black Belt is possibly up to three years. The need to make a distinction is obvious.

Which color is used for different belt ranks is a matter of choice by the individual school or system. Each system selects its color scheme and it is impossible to know what that rank signifies unless you know the requirements of the system. For instance, in Europe and parts of the United States, South America and Canada, the color scheme for Sport Judo is: White, Yellow, Orange, Green, Blue, Brown, Black, Red and White.

There are endless variations of the above scheme and the beginner should not be concerned over the differences which he will encounter. There are schools which even use light and dark shades of the same color to designate difference in rank. This is not the "wrong" way—it is simply their preference.

THE BLACK BELT

There are many misconceptions, prejudices and confusions concerning the holder of a Black Belt.

Some people actually believe that to become a Black Belt holder it is necessary to kill an opponent in combat!

Another misconception is that a Black Belt automatically qualifies its wearer as an instructor.

The Black Belt indicates a very high proficiency in performance.

Hard work, discipline, determination, physical and mental . . . and years of intense training precede the achievement of the Black Belt. It is a difficult achievement. It is the ultimate goal of the most able and serious student.

IS SPORT JUDO FOR SELF-DEFENSE?

It is misleading and dangerous to imply that Sport Judo training prepares a person for self-defense. Aside from the important fact that throwing techniques are not the best way to cope with common street attacks, the very method of training decreases their value further. In Sport Judo training, the partners approach, bow, grasp each other in prescribed fashion and attempt to maneuver each other into an off-balance position for throwing. Obviously, this cannot be done on the street. A street brawler has a better chance of throwing a fast punch than getting thrown. Granted that an exceptional individual with years of training in Sport Judo can apply throwing techniques in some self-defense situations—it is simpler, faster and more practical to learn the proper self-defense techniques. There is no sportsmanship in a street fight.

JAPANESE VOCABULARY

The use of Japanese terms has been kept to a minimum in this book. It is an imposition on the new student to ask him to learn a new language in order to learn a new art. A few years ago, it was necessary, for the simple reason that instructors who came here from Japan did not know English. Unlike fencing, which has retained a small vocabulary of French words for its international use, the Oriental unarmed arts for sport and self-defense have carried with them a heavy luggage of Japanese phrases on the journey over. The new student need not trouble himself with them. For those who want to learn all they can about Judo, the Japanese terms are given in the sections which list requirements for the belt degrees.

JUDO UNIFORM
HOW TO TIE THE BELT; CARE OF UNIFORM

The Japanese name for the Judo uniform is "gi," pronounced *gee* (with the "g" as in *go*). The use of the word "uniform" or "gi" is a matter of choice.

There is no important difference in brands of Judo uniforms. They differ from the Karate uniform in being much heavier in weight; the jacket of the Judo uniform is made of a double-weave material which is available only in the Japanese imported suits. The sizes are not given in U.S. standard clothes sizes, but in Judo numbers 1 to 5. Neither are the suits preshrunk, so that it is necessary to buy a uniform which is very large before being washed, so that it will fit properly after washing. There is considerable variation in the acceptable fit of the uniform; after washing, the sleeves of the jacket should come to about the middle of the forearm; if they come down to the wrist they are too long; if they come up to the elbow they are too short. The pants of the uniform are like drawstring pajamas and will fit almost any waist size; there is a small loop sewn onto the front of the pants through which you tie the drawstrings. The legs of the pants should come down about halfway on the shin; if they are somewhat shorter or longer it does not matter. Not being preshrunk, the uniform will be stiff and uncomfortable before being washed. A few washings and wearings will make it softer and more comfortable.

When ordering a uniform, give your height and weight, rather than your U.S. suit size, to make certain you order the correct size.

Except for the belt, the uniform should be washed in hot water and soap (the belt need not be washed). Traditionally, the Judo uniform is carefully folded when not in use and is carried in a small bag. A better way to take care of your uniform (avoiding mildew, allowing perspiration to dry) is to carry it on a hanger, or just loosely shaken out over your arm. Frequent washings are suggested out of consideration of other players and to prevent rotting from perspiration.

It is possible to practice without having a Judo uniform, though it is rather hard on ordinary clothes. If you do not have a Judo uniform, wear rugged clothes which give you complete freedom of movement. The sleeves should be sturdy enough to be gripped without danger of tearing, not only to avoid damage to your clothes, but to offer the support to the Receiver which he gets from maintaining his grip on your left sleeve as he takes his fall.

The belt of a Judo uniform goes around the body twice and ties in the front with a square knot; the end in your right hand goes over the end in your left hand and then goes under both thicknesses of the belt. Pull it snug; then put the left end over and around the end in your right hand, pull snug. Remember the sequence is: right over left, left over right.

KI-YA (SUPERPOWER)

Briefly stated, the principle of Ki-Ya (superpower) is the use of breath control simultaneously with the action. As you prepare to throw, inhale. As you execute the throw, exhale sharply and yell. The yell has the same effect as the grunt which you normally use when lifting or pushing a heavy object. It tenses the abdominal muscles for extra effort and concentrates extra power for the specific instant of action. The yell of Ki-Ya has an additional effect of startling and disconcerting the opponent.

Use of Ki-Ya has great value as a psychological contest technique. So effective is it that it was thought to have magical power in ancient times.

THE FALLS OF JUDO: A NEW APPROACH

Perhaps the most striking difference in my teaching methods from the old-fashioned ones is my approach to the Judo falling techniques.

The standard procedure of teaching Judo is to restrict the new student to learning only falling techniques for his first six months of training. As a discipline, this is acceptable. As a way of teaching it is contrary to all modern concepts. It makes the falls a dreary, repetitious and unpleasant part of learning Judo. I have reversed the procedure. Under my instruction, the student learns to throw at the same time that he learns to fall. Moreover, at my school it is considered a mark of advancement for a student to *receive* from a throw. It is actually easier to learn to throw than to receive. Newcomers are permitted to throw advanced students from the very beginning. When the new student has spent some time learning both throwing and falling techniques, then he is permitted to be thrown.

This method also frees the Judo student from an aversion to continuing practice of the falls for their own sake. I encourage the constant practice of the falls because they are excellent for exercise, coordination, suppleness and safety.

The basic and intermediate falls can be learned and done by anyone who will practice. The advanced falls are for those who wish to develop special skills and are not intended for the average student.

In practicing the falls, be certain that you have good form in the basic falls before going on to the intermediate falls. Do not attempt the advanced falls unless you have achieved excellent form in the intermediate falls.

Learning and practicing the falls with pleasure will be a great aid in beginning free-style Judo play. Students are commonly stiff and defensive if they have a worry about being thrown. If you have confidence in your ability to receive, you will find that you work in a more easy, relaxed manner and will enjoy the give and take of Judo play even when you are on the "wrong" end of a throw!

PRE-INSTRUCTION

The section which follows contains material which is basic to much of the instruction in the book. You should read and study it very carefully before you begin the practice of any of the techniques. Some of the material is very simple and some you will not be able to put to use until you have been practicing for a while. However, your *understanding* of it, even before you can apply it, is essential to a good foundation in Judo.

From time to time, especially as you begin each section of new work, you should reread the basic material. There are different ways of putting to use the various basic materials. You need only comprehend muscle reaction and body reaction to apply them to your practice from the very beginning. Pivots, on the other hand, should be practiced, when you are ready for them, as a continuing and never-ending part of Judo training. Even Black Belt players practice the pivots to keep in top training form.

As you become more experienced in your training, each rereading of the basic materials will mean more to you and will help you accelerate your progress.

HOW TO PRACTICE

Before you begin the actual practice of the techniques, *study* the book carefully. You should be acquainted with all the techniques before you do the physical training.

As you train, refer more than once to the written text and the photos. This is your method of correcting errors.

It is a good idea to keep a diary of your training. Keep track of the time spent on each lesson and note any difficulty you may have with particular techniques. In this way you will have a method for checking your rate of progress.

Rate of progress is a completely individual matter. It is impossible to tell how long it will take you to achieve a specific proficiency. It depends on your devotion, time spent, natural ability and body style. Do not let yourself get discouraged if your progress seems slow. Slow learning is not poor learning. On the contrary, a slow learner who is conscientious may retain what he has learned even better than a fast learner.

The general effects of this training are, for most people, extremely beneficial. You should get improved muscle tone, better coordination, suppleness, quickness of muscle reaction and improved breathing . . . if you are in normal good health. If you feel extreme muscle pain, exhaustion or any other symptom of body strain—check with a doctor. Only a doctor is qualified to diagnose your physical condition.

Your training program should be realistic and you should stick with it. It is better to practice at regular intervals for short periods of time than it is to neglect your training for weeks at a time and then try to cram it all into one long training period.

If your training time with your club, group or partner is very limited, you can accelerate your progress by regular and conscientious practice of the exercises which you can do alone.

SAFETY RULES FOR JUDO PRACTICE

When the rules of safety are followed, Judo is not a dangerous sport. During training and in practice sessions, the teacher, coach or group leader has the obligation to inform the players of specific safety rules and the added obligation of enforcing them.

THE FIRST RULE OF SAFETY: TAPPING FOR RELEASE

Judo players use a tapping signal for safety. Tapping is the signal for *immediate* release of any hold or choke. It is best to get into the habit of tapping your opponent, but you may tap yourself or the mat. Tapping is better than a verbal signal, for sometimes (as in a choke) you cannot easily talk or the sound is muffled. If you tap yourself, your partner may not notice the signal, but if you tap him, he will be aware that you are asking for release. It is dangerous and discourteous to maintain a hold or choke after the tapping signal.

In practice, when many techniques are done only to a certain point, tapping is also used to indicate "Stop," as, for instance, when partners practice taking to off-balance without completing the throw. It may also be used to indicate "Stop" by an instructor. *Tapping is the first rule of safety.*

Photos show tapping for release from chokes. In photo **1** it is convenient to tap the partner; in photo **2** it is more convenient to tap the mat.

THROWING SAFETY

When first learning to be thrown, students should *ease* each other to the mat, emphasizing form rather than speed. Speed is easy to acquire after the proper form is learned. When body throws are being practiced, the Receiver should *drag* his left arm across the Thrower's back making it act as a brake. Release of the dragging arm should be timed for slapping the mat properly. In beginning practice, Receiver should maintain a hold on Thrower's sleeve with his right hand. At the completion of the throw, Thrower should pull up on Receiver's right arm, providing an extra bit of brake on the fall.

In contest and free-style work players completely release each other upon completion of a throw. When fast throws are applied, the Thrower is in danger of being pulled down on top of the Receiver unless the release is quick. Both men could be hurt in this situation. However, if the Thrower intends to apply mat work after a throw, he does try to maintain a hold after the completion of certain throws for this purpose. The rule of safety is: Do not maintain a grip on your thrown opponent if it prevents him from taking a proper fall.

Until you have trained in the safety falls, do not allow yourself to be thrown. Until you can do the falls with ease and in the proper way, it is extremely dangerous to allow yourself to be thrown. Do not throw anyone who has not trained in the falling techniques.

Watch out for the other players. Learn to be alert when other players are working on the same mat. In free-style practice, no matter how large the mat area is, there is a possibility of throwing the Receiver into other players.

The proper throwing surface. Throwing and falling techniques should only be practiced on a mat, grass, sand or padded floor surface. Small gym mats are not suitable, unless they are taped or sewn together, as they tend to slide away from each other on a gym floor. Judo mats are expensive, and if you are working as a small group you will have to find or improvise a practice mat. If you have to work on a small mat, be careful about throwing your partner off the mat.

Men should always wear athletic supporters when practicing Judo.

DEGREE ETIQUETTE

Tell your degree. It is a form of courtesy, as well as a rule of safety, for players to exchange information before practicing together for the first time. If the players are not wearing colored belts which indicate rank, or if the color ranking system is one that is not familiar, they should tell each other how long they have trained and in what manner. Judo players who have not practiced together previously should work very slowly at first, to get acquainted with style of play. (Except, of course, in contest.)

ROUGH PLAY

Choking techniques should not be practiced by beginning students. Choking should be done only by those who have Brown Belt or higher degrees and only after they have learned how to revive an unconscious person, or in the presence of someone who knows how to revive an unconscious person. *Windpipe chokes are never allowed.*

Holding and locking techniques must be practiced with special care, slowly and with minimum pressure. The new student, who has less control of technique, must be particularly aware of the possibility of injury from chokes, holds and locks applied in a rough way.

Roughness in practice is discourteous, unsafe, and poor Judo procedure. You should decline to work with any person who is in the habit of "strong" play and who tries to substitute force for skill. An opponent who uses windpipe chokes, who does not release you on the tapping signal, whose style of work is needlessly violent, is subjecting you to possible injury and you are not required to submit to such behavior.

Don't be a guinea pig! In the old-fashioned style of Judo training, new students are actually used as fall guys for the advanced Judo players! This is not a sensible procedure. (It is a carryover from the ancient times when masters of the unarmed fighting arts used untrained peasants to practice on.) New students should not be thrown by advanced students; the opposite method is much better. Advanced students who have had experience in being thrown should be thrown by new students. New students who are throwing each other should do so only under the supervision of a coach or teacher. When new students are practicing without the benefit of supervision by teacher or coach, they should be extremely cautious and work very, very slowly to avoid accidents.

Self-defense techniques need not be practiced to the point of pain. These methods of self-defense have proven effective; you are not trying to make sure they work; you are only trying to learn them. Simulate the attack; practice the defense without hurting your partner. Kicks and hand blows should be stopped a few inches away from the intended target area. If you wish to practice actual hitting without hurting each other, you can do it in one of two ways:

1. Moderate blows can be done if you pad your arms and legs to protect them. You can use your imagination and available materials to make practice padding: toweling, flannel, or foam-rubber sheeting, for instance. Do *not* use pins to fasten padding material; use bandage clamps, or adhesive or plastic tape.

2. For practice of heavy blows, you can improvise a hanging bag using a laundry bag filled with sand, or you can pad any firm surface with towels or foam rubber.

Fingernails and toenails must be trimmed short and smooth. This is a courtesy and a safety measure.

EXERCISES: INTRODUCTION

If your main objective in practicing Judo is the exercise which it provides, you will find that it suits that purpose splendidly. Whatever additional exercises you do will depend on your practical situation (how much time you have available and what facilities you can use), your goals and interests (are you concentrating on Judo or do you prefer a variety of activities) and on your physical condition (what are the needs and limits of your body). There is a wide range of possibilities, from merely doing a few bending and stretching exercises to engaging in a heavy program of body conditioning, muscle developing and coordination-dexterity training. If you are with a group playing Judo for fun, you do not need to involve yourself in the same type of rigorous exercise and training as the player who intends to enter national competition.

The following are key exercises for suppleness, coordination and dexterity particularly useful for Judo players. If you have the time and inclination, other full-body activities (those which use the entire body action) such as walking, tennis and swimming are excellent to improve your over-all physical health. If you have particular weaknesses, you should choose additional activities which strengthen those areas: bicycling, for instance, for the legs; moderate weight work for the arms (avoid excessive weight training . . . heavy, slow muscles are not good for Judo).

Whether or not you have the ability to reach high proficiency in Judo, you should, if you enjoy it, continue your practice of it into advanced years for its exercise benefit. Exercise not only keeps you from feeling old; it keeps you from *being* old. Many ailments are now known to occur because of lack of regular exercise. Heart disease is more commonly the result of "loafer's heart" than it is of "athlete's heart." Exercise gives release from tension and results in psychological as well as physiological well-being.

WHEN YOU SHOULD GET ADVICE ABOUT EXERCISE

If you suffer from serious illness (chronic or acute), you should consult your doctor about the amount and type of exercise which is best for you. As you get older you should not give up exercise, though you may have to adjust the extent and kind of exercise you do.

Here are some signals which indicated that you should get advice from your doctor about your physical condition: If, after your exercise:

You are still very weak after two hours of rest.

Your heart pounds and you are breathless for more than ten
minutes.
You cannot sleep that night.
You are still tired the next day.

Only a doctor is qualified to tell if any of the above reactions are
due to a condition which requires limited or special exercise. It is
more probable that you need exercise badly and ought to start
slowly, gradually increasing the amount until you reach a normal,
health body state.

BODY TWIST

From a natural, relaxed stance, swing your arms and body from
side to side without moving your feet. Make the swinging action
vigorous, but not jerky.

3.   After you have done the above a few times, swing your arms
and upper body in one direction as you swing your leg in the opposite direction. Do this exercise a few times with one leg and
then with the other.

This is an excellent warming-up, loosening-up exercise.

BODY BENDING

4.   From a spread-leg stance, keeping your knees perfectly
straight, touch your head to one knee and then to the other. Anybody with a normal physique, in normal good health should be

3   4

able to do this exercise with a moderate amount of practice. Do not abuse your muscles and tendons by forcing. If you are very rigid and cannot bend easily, it will take some weeks to achieve the necessary suppleness. Regular practice for a few minutes each day will bring good results and there is no need to suffer strain or pain.

ROPE EXERCISE FOR ARM AND BODY THROWS

This is another of the training procedures which you can follow when your partner cannot practice with you. The aim is to perfect techniques of arm movement and coordinate them with leg and body movements.

In these photos the rope is held by a partner as a reference for you. In practice, you will fasten two lengths of rope to simulate arms. There is no equipment made for this purpose, so you will have to improvise with whatever materials you can. The ropes should be about two feet long; ends of the ropes should be fastened in such a way that you can exert considerable pull on them. Home-owners are ordinarily not enthusiastic about ropes attached to bedroom walls, so you had better look around for some acceptable garage or gym area for your rope project.

5.   Hold one end of the rope as though you were gripping your opponent at lapel area (standard practice position) and the other end as though you were gripping cloth at his sleeve.

6.   Practice the pivots (p. 50), pulling on the rope ends to simulate opponent's body resistance. Practice a variety of pivots.

7.   Practice a variety of leg throw positions (p. 103), using the rope to simulate resistance.

ISOMETRICS

The actions shown here are useful in developing a specific skill for free-style play: raising and lowering your opponent by arm and hand work.

8.   Partner shown right makes fists with both hands and holds them out, arms bent; partner shown left places his hands, palm down, on partner's fists. Both men take a deep breath, tighten abdomen; man at left presses down hard as partner opposes his push upward. Hold for the count of five, exhale and relax. Repeat five times.

9.   Partner shown right extends his arms, palms down. Left partner makes fists and places them under partner's extended hands. Both partners take deep breath, tighten abdomen; left partner pushes up hard with his fists as right partner opposes by pressing down. Hold for count of five. Exhale and relax. Repeat five times.

5

6

7

8

9   10

LEG STRETCH

10.   Start from a spread-leg stance, keeping bottoms of both feet flat on the mat; bend one knee, keeping the other leg extended and straight. Bend your knee as much as you can without taking the foot off the mat and without bending the knee of the extended leg. Do this exercise a few times, from side to side.

GLIDING—SLIDE STEPPING

No partner is required to practice this exercise. The second man is shown here merely as a reference point. The purpose of this exercise is to improve balance and develop lightness of movement. While it helps you with Judo and Karate work, it also increases your general body control, enabling you to do other work and play without awkwardness.

11.   From a relaxed "T" stance, place most of your weight on your rear (left) foot.

12.   Take a light step out with your right foot.

13.   Place your weight down on your right foot and *slide* your left foot forward so that you are in a "T" stance with weight on your forward foot.

14.   Take a light step back with your left foot. Place your weight on your left foot and then slide your right foot back so that you are in the starting position.

11

12

13

14

Your arms and upper body remain relaxed throughout; the movement is only in the legs. Keep the step and glide light and smooth.

In addition to practicing the step and glide forward and back, practice step gliding from side to side and then in random ways (to approximate the kinds of steps you might take in free-style work).

EIGHT-COUNT HOP

In free-style and contest play, it is very important that you move on your feet easily, quickly and without loss of balance. This is an exercise to train you in graceful movement and shifting of body weight.

Mark an X on the mat. The foot which bears your weight should be on the X throughout the eight counts.

15.   Starting position, hands on hips, weight on left foot (on X), right foot extended with slight weight on ball of foot.

16.   Hop lightly, placing your weight on right foot (on X), left foot extended.

17.   Return to starting position.

18.   Hop lightly onto your right foot, your left foot is extended back.

19.   Hop lightly onto your left foot, your right foot is extended back.

15   16

17

18

19

20

20. Hop lightly onto your right foot, your left foot is extended forward.

21. Hop lightly onto your left foot, your right foot is extended forward.

22. Hop lightly onto your right foot, your left foot is extended to the side.

23. Hop lightly onto your left foot, your right foot is extended to the side (as in starting position).

24, 25. Show how this exercise is applied in Judo. 24. Left player attempts unsuccessful Sweeping Foot Throw (p. 103) and

25, he lightly hops to the other foot to follow quickly with a Sweeping Foot Throw on the other side.

ROLLING FORWARD AND BACKWARD

26. Start from seated position.

27. Roll back and place your hands on the mat, palms up, twisting your head to one side as you roll.

21   22

23

24

25

26

27

28. Going over, your hands will brace you (now palms down) and the rolling momentum of your legs will help you complete the roll.

29. Finish the roll in a kneeling position.

30. Rise into squatting position.

31. Tuck your head well in and roll forward. End in seated position. Practice the rolling exercise backward and forward a few times.

28

29

30

31

NECK-BODY TWIST

Especially useful for strengthening the neck, this is a standard Judo exercise. It is excellent for increasing your ability to bridge and roll and will improve your mat work. It is a difficult exercise, so do not be discouraged if you must put time and hard work into it.

32. Throughout the exercise, neither your hands nor hips touch the mat. Start with hands behind your back, head on the mat, legs spread with weight on balls of feet.

33. Cross one leg over the other and pivot on the top of your head.

34. With weight only on your feet and head, roll over into position shown. From this position, cross one leg over the other and roll back into starting position. With practice, you should be able to execute a continuous rolling from back to front position, rolling first in one direction and then rolling back.

32

33

34

35   36

PRACTICE AND CONTEST STANCES
PRACTICE STANCE

35.   For training purposes, the standard position for practicing throws is from this stance: both players stand facing, feet are about shoulder width apart; each player holds opponent's jacket at the lapel area with a natural grip. (Get a good grip onto the jacket at the reinforced edge.) Each player's left hand grips cloth at the underside of opponent's right arm between the elbow and shoulder area.

36.   For contest, it is better to bend the knees, giving your body a lower center of gravity.

37

BODY MECHANICS

We show how a lighter person can hold the weight of a heavier, larger person.

37. A light person can hold (or balance for throwing) a heavier person with ease when weight distribution is correct and balance is proper. To balance a larger person, stand with your feet about shoulder width apart, with knees slightly bent. Keeping the lower part of the body in a straight line, bend the upper body to the left *from the waist only*. Experiment with your partner to find the perfect position for easy balancing. Let your partner stand behind you and when you have assumed the position described above, put your arm around his waist and let him topple himself onto your back and hip. Do not *lift* him with your arms; merely guide him into position.

Check for corrections: Knees bent slightly; feet about shoulder width apart; upper body bent considerably to the left (jutting out the right hip) without letting the knees close in. You should be able to hold a heavier, bigger person in balance *with ease* before you start practice of the body throws.

BALANCES

In the normal standing position, your body is in very weak balance. To demonstrate, stand with your legs about shoulder width apart,

38   39

arms at your sides 38 and let your partner push at you from the side. If you stand firmly, you can resist his push fairly well. Next, let your partner pull you forward 39 and push you backward 40. It is impossible for you to maintain balance in these two instances. It requires only slight push or pull effort to take you completely off balance.

41.   Next, take a conventional boxing stance and let your partner push at you from the side. Again, you can resist his sideward push fairly well. But, when he pushes you backward 42 or pulls you forward, you cannot resist. In a boxing stance, only the angle of resistance has changed.

43.   The weakest of all balances is the one-point balance. From this position, you are vulnerable to the slightest push or pull from any and to any angle. This is the balance which you are in whenever you walk, or shift from one foot to the other.

40

41

42

43

44   45

The strongest balance you can take is the "T" position 44. A "T"
position can be taken with the right or left foot forward. Shown
here, the left foot is forward and the right foot is held at a 90°
angle to the forward foot. This is the same stance which is used by
fencers. In this position you are able to resist a sideward push or
pull and you can better resist a forward or backward push or pull
45 than from a natural or boxer's stance. For self-defense, there
is an added advantage to taking the "T" position when facing an
adversary—because of the cant of your body, you offer less target
area.

CANTING

Imagine that you are following the outside rim of a circle with
your hands.

46. With your right hand and arm, pull on Receiver's cloth, up
and over (following the top half of the imaginary circle rim) and
with your left hand, pull down and around (following the bottom
half of the circle rim). Practice the canting action to the opposite
direction as well.

Canting changes the alignment of the Receiver's body; it weakens
his balance and makes him move in an awkward manner.

46

47

48

TILTING

47, 48. Tilting has much the same objective as canting; canting involves the wheeling action, while tilting involves the simpler procedure of pulling forward, pushing backward or to any angle which weakens Receiver's balance and places him in an awkward position, vulnerable for your intended throw.

COMBINATION CANTING, TILTING AND LIFTING

Now you will apply several of the actions which weaken your opponent, interfere with his balance, raise his center of gravity and make him increasingly vulnerable to being thrown.

49 ←

50 →

51 ←

52 →

49, 50. Using a continuous and gradual pressure, pull your opponent up onto the balls of his feet and continue the upward lift as you tilt and twist (cant) him. Practice doing this to all directions so that you learn to control your opponent and weaken his resistance to your attempted throws. Working with the *idea* of control, shifting and changing your canting, tilting, lifting actions to suit the requirement of your relative positions, will take you out of the category of defensive man and will help to make you a versatile and active Judo player.

BODY REACTION

Body reaction is the action of the body which automatically opposes a force against it. Make this experiment with a friend. (Do not tell him what you are attempting to prove.) Grasp his lapel or any cloth at upper chest height and pull forward until you feel his strong resistance back. When his resistance is strong, quickly *push* back and you will find his body easily moving back out of balance. His former resistance gives additional power to your push.

51. To set up the Receiver for a forward throw, push him backward until you feel that he is resisting your backward push (by moving forward).

52. Using Receiver's reaction, pull him sharply forward into position to execute a forward throw.

You set up Receiver for a backward throw by pulling him forward and slightly up. As he resists the forward pull, use his reaction to push him backward into position for a backward throw.

Body reaction can be utilized from side to side and at any angle. The basic principle is always the same; push or pull Receiver in the *opposite* direction you need him to move for the ending throw. If your opponent is very strong, you may have to use several feinting actions before he will react in the direction which makes him vulnerable to your intended throw.

MUSCLE REACTION

Muscle reaction and body reaction are based on the same general idea. Ordinarily, our bodies resist any forceful movement by opposing that force in the opposite direction. Muscle reaction is merely more specific than body reaction.

53

54

55

56

53. Forcefully push down on your partner's extended fist while he resists your push by trying to push up.

54. If you *suddenly* stop pushing, his fist will jerk upward without any effort on your part. If you are holding his fist and suddenly stop your downward push and reverse the direction to an upward pull, you can pull his captured fist high with very little effort on your part. The Judo idea of "going with" your opponent, rather than "opposing" him, does not mean that you allow your opponent to do anything he wants to do, but rather that you manipulate him into doing what you want him to do by using his own force to your advantage.

USING OPPONENT'S STRENGTH

55. If a heavier person pushes with all his weight and force against a lighter person, the lighter person has no chance of successfully opposing the push. Shown here I am pushing my 200 pounds of weight against Elise's 100, a double amount of force.

56. Since she cannot *oppose* my 200 pounds with her 100 pounds, she pulls me in the direction I am pushing. This gives a 200 pound pushing and a 100 pound pulling force going in the same direction, so that I actually move with 300 pounds of force.

FOLLOWTHROUGH ARM WORK

Most throws require a *combination* of actions (arm, leg and body work). A common error of beginning Judo players is the omission of the final element—arm-work followthrough. When you include the final step of arm work, you insure a crisp technique which will convince the judges that you have had your opponent under control completely. Otherwise, you may break his balance and trip him down, but the resulting sloppy throw lacks the sparkle which is characteristic of good throwing technique.

For training purposes, only the arm-work portion of the throw is shown here, to illustrate the shift in arm movement direction.

57. You have Receiver in off-balance position and you have canted his body so that he is set up for your throw.

58. When the throw has been applied and Receiver is on the way down, insure a crisp throw by following through with arm movement; your right hand and arm force him around and down into the mat as your left hand and arm pull straight back sharply; your upper body follows and assists the arm action.

SHADOW THROWING
PRACTICE OF THROWING FORM

To accelerate your training, you can practice many of the techniques without your partner. The more often you "walk through" the action of throwing, the better your technique will become. You practice the form of throwing as though with a partner. In the same manner that a boxer shadow-boxes you can shadow-throw. The photos showing the action with a partner are for reference only so that you can compare each stage of the throw with its shadow action.

You can also practice the essential preliminary actions for throwing if you use a partner whom you *cannot* throw (because there is no suitable surface for falling or because he does not have training in how to fall). Moving in for the throw with speed and grace is the most important part of your training. If you cannot move into position quickly, your opponent will not be there for you to throw. If you move in awkwardly, you will not be in strong throwing position. When you practice with a partner who cannot be thrown, do the actions up to the point of the throw. It is excellent training procedure.

59, 60. Take standard beginning position.

61, 62. Pivot.

63, 64.   Balance your shadow opponent. (When practicing with a partner who cannot be thrown, avoid taking him to this balance too vigorously or he may go over accidentally.)

65, 66.   With arm and body movement, follow through.

67, 68.   Take strong ending position.

63

64

65

66

67   68

FOOTWORK

Good habits of foot movement must be developed from the very
beginning of your Judo practice. Your normal walking steps are
not appropriate for Judo; in normal walking you are on one-point
balance too much of the time and vulnerable to being thrown.
Proper Judo footwork keeps you strongly balanced, lets you move
more rapidly without getting into awkward positions and allows
you to control your opponent more easily.

As you move about on the mat in free-style practice, use gliding-
sliding steps on the balls of the feet. Weight should be equally
divided on both feet; keep your feet at least six inches apart; do
not cross your feet; do not lift your feet (except, of course, when
applying a throw); when your opponent moves your body, do not
oppose his movement by stepping away from it, but drag your feet
in the direction he is pulling and try to use the same directional
movement to your own advantage. As you position your opponent,
use the steps as an essential part of the action. (See Gliding—Slide
Stepping, p. 28 .)

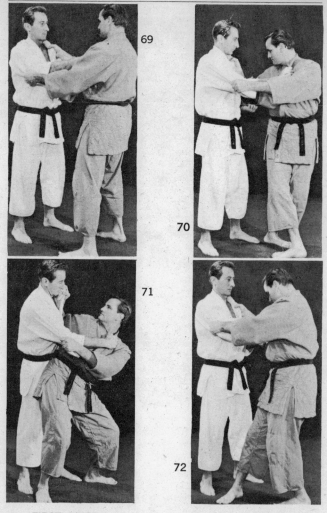

FIRST PIVOT

69. Players start from standard position, Thrower shown right.

70. You slide your left foot in a half circle, placing it in front of Receiver's left foot with your toes pointing away from him. Your body turns to follow the movement of the pivot.

71.   Keeping your left foot in place, complete the body turn to place yourself directly in front of Receiver and step with your right foot to place it in front of Receiver's right foot. At the completion of the pivot, both your feet should be directly in front of his feet.

SECOND PIVOT

Players begin in standard position, Thrower shown right.

72.   You step cross body with your right foot, placing it in front of Receiver's right foot; toes point away from him, weight is carried only on the ball of the foot.

73.   Pivoting on the ball of the right foot, turn your body counterclockwise to place yourself directly in front of Receiver, your feet in front of his feet.

THIRD PIVOT

Players begin in standard postion, Thrower shown right.

74.   Step cross body with your left foot, placing it in front of Receiver's left foot, toes pointing toward him, with your weight carried only on the ball of the foot.

73
←

74
→

75

76

77

78

75. Pivoting on the ball of your left foot, turn your body counterclockwise and place yourself directly in front of Receiver, both your feet in front of his feet.

FOURTH PIVOT

76. Players are facing, Thrower, shown right, is positioned to the left side of Receiver; your left foot in front of his left foot.

77. Pivoting on the ball of your left foot, turn your body counterclockwise to place yourself directly in front of Receiver.

FIFTH PIVOT

78. Players are facing, Thrower shown right; your right foot is in front of Receiver's right foot.

79. Pivoting on the ball of your right foot, back in (turning your body counterclockwise) to place yourself directly in front of him.

SIXTH PIVOT
(TWO-FOOT LEAPING PIVOT)

80. Players are facing, Thrower is not close in to Receiver.

79

80

81, 82.   Springing from the balls of both feet, you leap and twist your body (counterclockwise) to place yourself directly in front of Receiver.

SEVENTH PIVOT

(ONE-FOOT LEAPING PIVOT)

Players stand facing, Thrower is not close in to Receiver.

83, 84.   Springing off from the ball of the left foot, leap onto your left foot directly in front of Receiver with your right leg bent (as shown) in position to execute throws appropriate for this ending. You can also end the one-foot leap with your right leg straight, in position to execute appropriate throws.

SLOW-MOTION ANALYSIS OF THROWS

To help you understand the essential action of the throws, the text and photos present them as though they were stopped several times from beginning to end to show you how they work. When you first begin practice of any of the throws, you must do them in very slow-motion. You may actually hesitate between the different "parts" of the throw. Later, in order to do the throw properly, you must blend the "steps" so that there is no hesitation between them; so that the different parts merge into one smooth, flowing action. It is much better to concentrate on technique than on speed. When your technical ability to do a throw is good, then you can increase your speed.

In some of the throws (for instance, Sweeping Loin) the throw is much more difficult to perform in slow-motion than when you have the impetus of both bodies moving to assist you. Even so, if you can do such throws in slow-motion you will eventually achieve a greater degree of expertness.

Many of the throws can be practiced with a beginning partner who cannot receive! Note that there are throws in which the action involving the greatest skill is that part *leading up to* the actual throw. If you find yourself in a situation where you do not have a partner who can receive, both of you should practice first steps of all the techniques in preparation for continuing the work under more suitable conditions.

I caution you again—do not throw anyone who has not been trained in the falling techniques and do not allow yourself to be thrown until you know the falls for safety!

81 ←

82 →

83 ←

84 →

PROCEDURE FOR TESTS

FORMAL THROWING FOR BELT DEGREES:

Formal throwing is stylized, prearranged demonstration of technical skill. Unlike free-style practice or contest, players do not oppose each other. However, they do not merely *fall down*; they offer no resistance and allow themselves to be thrown if the throw is executed properly.

Details of the test procedure will vary from school to school, from club to club and from instructor to instructor. Since the technical skill of the player (or players) will be judged by a Judo degree holder of superior rank, he will decide the exact procedure to be followed. My method is offered here as a guide.

Students are permitted to demonstrate formal throws for degree advancement when, in the opinion of the teacher or coach, they are ready for the test. Sometimes, a student will be given a short preliminary test to determine his readiness. Very often, two students who are working for the same degree promotion will practice together and demonstrate the formal throws together. Since this is a test of technical skill, both players may be advanced in degree upon demonstration of required techniques.

At my school, the ceremony for demonstrating formal throws has been simplified to a bow at the beginning and at the end of the formal test.

Players stand facing each other about six feet apart, bow, then take short steps in unison until they are close enough to grip. They hesitate, then grasp each other in the standard manner for throwing. The Thrower initiates the beginning of the actual throw, by a nod of his head. At his signal, both players take several steps in unison and the Thrower executes the throw. The number of steps and the direction in which they are taken will depend on the throw being demonstrated. It should be part of the practice procedure (for the test) that the steps are counted and prearranged. Taking the steps gives both players a bit of momentum which assists the execution of a good throw and a good fall. The rhythm of the steps adds to the gracefulness of the players and makes for a handsome and elegant demonstration.

After the demonstration of each throw, the players rise to face each other and proceed to the next technique (without a bow). For each throw, the student is judged on his ability to execute the throw and for the ability to receive from the throw. Thus, even if only one of the students is taking the test, each throw is done twice, once to determine throwing ability and once to determine technique as the Receiver.

The falls are also demonstrated in formal fashion for advancement in degree. Falls which are done for formal demonstration should be practiced with steps preceding them. The number of steps and the direction in which they are taken vary according to the fall and according to the style preferred by the coach or teacher.

HONORARY, FORM, WOMEN'S AND JUNIOR DEGREES

It is the practice of many Judo organizations to issue degrees in Judo for accomplishments other than contest skill. At the discretion of the instructor, degrees may be given for superior accomplishment in form work (Kata), for ability in teaching, or for services in promoting and furthering the art.

Degrees for services rendered are honorary degrees and may be compared to the honorary degrees given by universities to outstanding citizens or scholars.

Form and instruction degrees are proficiency degrees and represent high achievement in the art of Judo (though the wearer of the degree may not be trained for contest).

It is customary for women to earn Judo degrees in form work, although they may have a knowledge of contest. It has been my experience that women can learn and enjoy Judo forms and reach a strong level of competence. Very few women can (or care to) engage in Contest Judo with a great degree of skill. Form Judo degrees are a fine way of encouraging women to participate in the wonderful fun of Sport Judo.

A white stripe is usually sewn down the length of women's belts.

Ordinarily, there are different colors for belt degrees given to juniors. Age 16 is the minimum age for earning adult degrees. The requirements may be the same, or similar, but the color of the belt indicates that it is a junior degree. Blue (or pale violet) is commonly used to indicate junior Brown Belt and purple is used to indicate junior Black Belt. It is also possible to indicate special and junior degrees by using various patches sewn on the belt, or a strip of blue or purple sewn the length of the adult color belt.

INDIVIDUAL STYLE OF JUDO PLAY

Before you can think of developing your own style of Judo play, you must first learn to do the throws well in the manner taught by your instructor. Until you can do this, you have no way of assessing the difference between an error and a stylistic improvement. When you can perform in the conventional, or required style, then you can begin to probe the possibilities of variation which might improve your ability.

The old-style method of teaching makes very little allowance for differences in individuals. Since we all have different body styles, physiques and temperaments, we must acknowledge the value of adjusting Judo work to suit the individual. Not only are there different techniques which are best for a small man or a large man, but the question of individual *preference* is very important. If certain techniques work for you, they are the best for you; if changing a technique makes it work better for you, make the change!

To acquire a balanced repertory of work, select one main throw and several secondary throws, then make these your principal contest techniques. No one can advise you better than your own judgment as to the selection of these throws. Whatever *works* best and *feels* best is *your* best choice. When you have selected these main throws, practice them to perfecton. *But*, do not make the mistake of giving up the practice of other throws.

The Judo man who learns one or two throws to perfection and uses *only* these few techniques in contest may be a sure winner, but he is not an accomplished Judo player. If the purpose of playing is exclusively to win contest, the single-throw champion is acceptable. A better player is one who has a greater variety of throws at his command, who can vary his play as the opponents vary, who can take advantage of "by-chance" opportunities and who uses the fullest repertory of the art which his individual body style can accommodate.

In Judo as in many other sports, the really great champions have been those whose style of work is unique. Conformity makes for mediocrity in physical work as in mental work. If you have the discipline to work hard and the courage to be an individual, you will achieve the highest degree of competence.

PART TWO

Falls, Throws, Free-Style Practice, and Formal Demonstrations for Belt Degrees

GREEN BELT REQUIREMENTS AND TRAINING

For advancement to the rank of Green Belt (4th kyu or yonkyu), it is necessary to demonstrate in the formal manner the throws and falls taught in this section:

GREEN BELT FALLS (ukemi)

1. Back Fall
2. Side Fall
3. Basic Side Roll
4. Intermediate Back Fall
5. Basic Forward Roll
6. Forward Roll—Coming Up
7. Intermediate Side Roll—Coming Up
8. Intermediate Side Roll—Leaping
9. Intermediate Side Fall
10. Forward Fall

GREEN BELT THROWING (nage waza)

AND RECEIVING THROWS (ukemi)

1. Hip Throw (tsurikomi goshi)
2. Neck Throw (koshi guruma)
3. Over-Shoulder Throw (seoi nage)
4. One-Arm Over-Shoulder Throw (ippon seoi nage)
5. Kickback Throw (o-soto gari)
6. Straight Foot Throw (tai otoshi)
7. Lateral Dash Throw (uki waza)
8. Circle Throw (tomoe nage)

It is also necessary to demonstrate some ability in Free-Style Exercise (randori).

All the material in this section should be studied, though the formal test will not include it all. The additional training is given so that you can get a strong foundation while learning the Green Belt work and are well prepared for continuing your training toward the higher degrees.

ADDITIONAL TRAINING—NOT REQUIRED FOR TEST

Salutation Bow and the Courtesy Throw
Tips for Tall Men
Tips for Short Men
Counters Against Stiff-Arming
How to Block Throws
Tactical Use of Throws for Free-Style Practice and Contest

GREEN BELT FALLS

NUMBER ONE FALL, BACK FALL

85. Start from seated position, hands on knees, head slightly forward.

86. Fall *gently* back with a rolling (not *thrusting*) motion, raising hands to get more power in the slap. Keep body slightly curled.

87. Finish by slapping the mat with force, just before the upper back touches the mat. Head *never* hits the mat. Avoid jerking back into the fall. Hit the mat with the palms of the hands with arms fully extended and fairly close into the body. Slapping absorbs impact and allows you to fall with less jarring action to the back and to the internal organs. Hands are very slightly cupped.

NUMBER TWO FALL, SIDE FALL

88. Starting position: lying flat on back, head off the mat, arms held in front of face.

89. This fall is practiced from side to side. Shown here, the fall is started to the left side. As the body rolls to the left side, the right foot is swung over and the left hand makes a wide arc to add power to the slap. As the body is completely rolled onto the side, the left hand and the bottom of the right foot hit the mat at the same time. Hand and foot slap the mat with force to absorb impact. Head never touches the mat. Arm is fully extended and slaps in fairly close to body. From this position, roll over to right side, right hand and bottom of left foot slapping mat at the same time. Repeat from side to side. Be sure to keep bottom leg straight and head off the mat.

My preference for the crossed-over leg ending is based on its safety. The groin is protected by the crossed-over leg; there is less danger of injury if Thrower should lose his balance and fall onto Receiver; in a fast throw there is less likelihood of continuing to roll because the crossed-over leg acts as a brace; less possibility of landing on tailbone; groundwork is more difficult for Thrower to execute if Receiver has crossed-over leg.

90, 91. Photos show variations of #2 fall which are technically correct and preferred by some instructors, but do not have safety value of crossed-over leg ending.

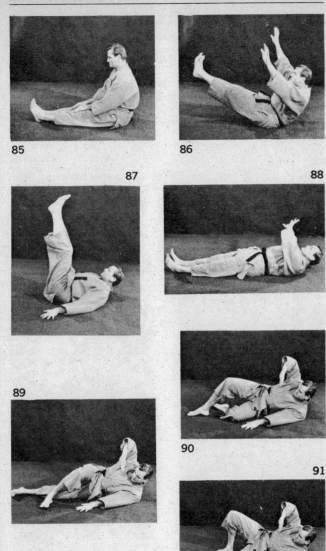

85

86

87

88

89

90

91

92.   Sometimes #2 fall is practiced with the legs held up and only the upper body rolling from side to side.

NUMBER THREE FALL, BASIC SIDE ROLL

93.   Feet are placed about shoulder width apart and on a straight line. (For beginners, draw a straight line on the mat and place the toes at the line.) First, place the right hand directly in front of you, fingers pointing straight ahead. Feet and right hand form a triangle. Place left hand directly in the center of triangle, fingers pointing to your right foot; left elbow points away from body at a 45° angle.

94.   Think of an imaginary line which extends from your left shoulder to your right hip. This will be the line of your fall. Shift your weight to your right hand and left foot, raising your right foot so that you begin to lose your balance.

95, 96.   Remembering the line of your fall, continue the roll along your left arm and shoulder, across your back and ending on your right side, slapping with right hand and bottom of left foot

92
←

93
→

94
←

95
→

as you finish the roll. The ending position is exactly the same as for #2 fall.

Avoid going straight over as in a somersault. Tuck the head well in at the beginning of the roll. This should be a gentle, rolling fall; all the force should be in the ending slap with the rest of the body relaxed, not rigid. Improper falling will be felt mainly in the shoulder. With practice there should be no sensation of jarring the shoulder. Practice for smoothness first, not speed.

NUMBER FOUR FALL, INTERMEDIATE BACK FALL

Start from relaxed standing position, arms extended forward.

97.   Lean forward, as though to touch toes, as you shift all your weight to your right foot.

98.   Extending your left foot, sit down *as close as possible* to your right heel and raise your arms.

99.   When your body is as close to the mat as possible, lose your balance backward, slap the mat with force with both palms and

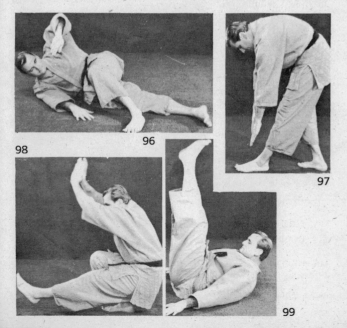

96

98

97

99

raise your legs. Head never touches the mat. Avoid thrusting yourself backward; use a rolling motion. If you have brought your body
close enough to the mat in photo 98, you will be able to finish
properly. Keep the hands slightly cupped, spread fingers for most
forceful slap.

NUMBER FIVE FALL, BASIC FORWARD ROLL

100.   Start with feet about shoulder width apart; body squatting
down low to the mat; hands in front of feet, palms down, fingers
pointing out to sides.

101.   Tuck head in, shift weight onto hands, roll over.

102.   End with both hands and feet hitting mat at the same time,
hands slapping with force; hips and head do not hit mat at all;
knees are sharply bent at finish.

Avoid letting hips touch the mat at any time in this fall; head does
not touch mat at finish.

NUMBER SIX FALL, FORWARD ROLL—COMING UP

Start from relaxed standing position, arms folded on top of head.
Beginners should keep feet wide apart.

103.   Squat low to the mat.

104.   Keeping the arms on top of head, roll over.

105.   Continue the roll, thrusting hands outward to help you up
to a standing position. Placing the feet wide apart at the end of the
roll will help the beginner continue to a standing position.

NUMBER SEVEN FALL, INTERMEDIATE SIDE ROLL—
COMING UP

The rolling-over action in this fall is the same as for #3 fall. The
difference is in the beginning and ending.

100

101

102

103

104

105

C

106.   Placing hands in front of you as shown, take a step with your left foot. Lead with left elbow.

107.   Place hands on the mat, raise right foot and begin the roll over, keeping right leg bent as you roll.

108.   Slap with force with your right hand and continue the roll, using the right hand and forward momentum to propel you upward.

109.   Finish in a standing "T" position, facing the place where you started the fall.

Avoid jarring the shoulder; a smooth slow rolling motion is what you are aiming for, not speed, at first. Tuck your head well in as you roll.

106

107

108

109

110.   111.

112.   113.

NUMBER EIGHT FALL, INTERMEDIATE SIDE ROLL—LEAPING

110.   When you can do #7 fall smoothly and well, continue on to practice #8, which has similar motion, except that it is done with several steps and a leap. Form fists with the hands and use sides of fists on mat, rather than placing hands down as in #7. Begin practice of #8 fall by leaping over very small objects and progress to greatest height you can achieve.

NUMBER NINE FALL, INTERMEDIATE SIDE FALL

111.   Point right foot to the side and swing left arm back.

112, 113.   Raise left foot and swing left leg cross-body as left hand swings in same direction (palm down) while lowering body as close as possible to right heel.

114.   When body is very close to mat, fall onto left side with rolling motion, bringing both legs up and slapping with left hand.

Remember, this is a side (not a back) fall; finish should be well onto the side. Practice falling onto the right side as well.

NUMBER TEN FALL, FORWARD FALL

115.   Beginner's starting position, on knees; hands are swung up in front of face, palms outward.

116.   Lose balance forward, slapping mat with entire area of arms from forearm to hands. Hands slap first, then the forearm. Hands are directly in front of face at finish; elbows point slightly outward.

117.   Advanced student's starting position, standing; legs spread, hands swung up in front of face.

114

115

116

117

118

119

120

118. Fall directly forward, entire body is off mat at the finish except for toes, forearms and hands.

Avoid catching the mat with wrists bent.

This fall is widely taught in Judo, but has no Sport Judo application. It is a safety fall in the event of tripping or being pushed forward.

GREEN BELT THROWS
HIP THROW (BASIC BODY THROW)

119. Standard beginning position. Thrower shown facing rear.

120. Thrower begins back-in pivot by stepping with his left foot, placing it in back of his right foot, toes pointing in opposite direction, as shown. (This is the fifth position in ballet.) For beginning practice purposes, do not move the right foot while this action is made. The body will turn in the proper direction simply because of the changed position of the feet.

121. The back-in pivot is completed by turning counterclockwise as you step with the right foot, ending with your feet directly in front of the Receiver's feet. Your left-hand grip remains as it was, the right hand goes around Receiver's waist as you make the pivot. Bend the upper body sharply to the left and bend knees slightly. Your hip should be placed at Receiver's thighs.

122.* When you can execute the pivot well, it will be a smooth, continuous motion. Maintain both hand grips as you pivot, placing your right elbow in Receiver's armpit as you turn.

123. To execute the throw, pull around with your left hand as you lift up with your right arm (if the arm is around the waist) or lever up with your right elbow; continue the twisting of your arms as you spring up with a slight straightening of your legs, turning your body to your left.

124. When Receiver is on the way over (not before his weight has left your hip) release the right-hand grip, step back with your right foot into a "T" position and pull up firmly with your left hand. Receiver maintains hold with his right hand, slapping with his left hand.

Because this is the basic body throw, it is important to learn it very well. You will then find that the other body throws which are based on it will be much easier to learn. Using the arm-around-the-waist position for learning practice has value for the Thrower and for the Receiver. The Thrower will find it easier to balance the Receiver and he can execute the pivot more easily (though more slowly). The Receiver is helped to take an easier fall when the arm is around his waist. This is extremely important when both Receiver and Thrower are of equal proficiency.

Progress to the position in photo 122 can be made when the Thrower is able to execute the pivot quickly and when the Receiver is able to take a faster throw with safety.

When this throw is used in contest, Thrower will release both hand grips as the throw is completed and will take a step back completely free of the Receiver. This makes the point clear and obvious and will keep the Receiver from dragging the Thrower down with the momentum of his fall.

*Note: As a beginner, practice Hip Throw with arm around the waist as shown in photo 121. However, standard Hip Throw form is as shown in photo 122.

121

122

123

124

NECK THROW

Neck Throw is similar to Hip Throw in the major actions. Beginning stance is standard. The *back-in pivot* is used.

125.   As the pivot is made, Thrower places his right arm around Receiver's neck.

126.   Receiver is brought to balance with the same body and leg action as for Hip Throw, but the Thrower's entire right arm acts to lever Receiver around and down.

127.   As the throw is completed, Thrower's levering right arm follows the action until the moment when Receiver actually leaves his hip.

This throw is required for achieving Green Belt. In contest, it is useful against a taller opponent. (See Tips for Tall and Short Men, p. 82.)

OVER-SHOULDER THROW

The major actions are the same as for Hip Throw. Beginning position is standard and the *back-in pivot* is used.

128.   As the pivot is executed, both hands of the Thrower maintain their grip and his right elbow locks into Receiver's right armpit. The variation from the basic Hip Throw (advanced style) is that the elbow is placed under the right, rather than the left, armpit of Receiver.

The throw is executed in the same manner as Hip Throw, with the right elbow lifting up and then around and down to assist the body and leg actions.

The advantage of this variation is that there is no shifting of hand position, making it a quicker throw. It is easy to get into a good, strong, low throwing position in this variation and the Receiver takes a higher (more spectacular) fall.

ONE-ARM OVER-SHOULDER THROW

The basic actions for this throw are the same as for Hip Throw. Beginning is standard and the *back-in pivot* is used.

125   126

127   128

129   130

129, 130.   As the pivot is executed, Thrower drops his right arm down and then brings it into proper position gripping outside of Receiver's right arm at the shoulder. Throw is executed in same manner as Over-Shoulder Throw.

The most common mistake made in practicing this throw is failing to drop the right arm *down*, before taking the shoulder grip. Unless the arm is dropped down and straight, it will not move freely into position.

KICKBACK THROW

131.   Standard beginning position.

132.   Thrower takes a deep step with his left foot and places it beside Receiver's right foot. As the step is taken, Thrower cants Receiver into off-balance position by pushing around and down with his right arm and pulling backward and down with his left hand.

133, 134.   Continuing the push-pull action with his arms, Thrower raises his right leg and kicks with his calf at Receiver's right calf.

131

132

133

134

135   **136**

135, 136. Follow through is shown as Thrower kicks Receiver's leg up and continues the arm motion which completes the throwing action.

Avoid the common error of attempting to *push* Receiver's leg with your leg. The action is snappy and Thower's leg is kept firm and straight. Unless Receiver is canted into one-point balance by the arm motion, the throw will not be successful, for even if you kick his leg out from under him, he remains standing on the other leg and you will find yourself "wrestling" him down with force. The "easy way" requires *continuous* arm motion and a snappy kick.

This throw is one of the easiest for new students to learn and it can be adapted to practical use for self-defense.

STRAIGHT FOOT THROW

Standard beginning position.

137. Thrower uses a pivot similar to (not exactly like) *step-in pivot*, pointing his left foot away from Receiver and at a 45° angle to the direction Receiver faces. As the pivot is begun, Thrower pulls Receiver forward into his chest with both arms.

138. Placing most of his weight on left leg, Thrower locks his right leg ankle-to-ankle against Receiver's right foot.

139. As this leg action is being done, Thrower turns his body to his left as he pulls back and down with his left arm and around and down with his right arm. Thrower's body is following a circular motion.

140. Throw is completed with a sharp and snappy body and arm twist.

Avoid the common error of bending the right leg and be sure to place it *ankle-to-ankle*. Arms should pull Receiver in close, actually into Thrower's chest. The right leg remains in place until Receiver is on the way down, only then does Thrower step back into his "T" position.

137

138

139

140

LATERAL DASH THROW

Standard beginning position.

141.   Thrower pivots on ball of left foot so that his toes point at a 45° angle toward Receiver as he places his right foot on Receiver's left instep. As this footwork is begun, Thrower tilts Receiver forward and clockwise with arm movement.

142.   Pulling forward with both arms, Thrower starts to place himself on the ground off to the right side of Receiver.

141

142

143

144

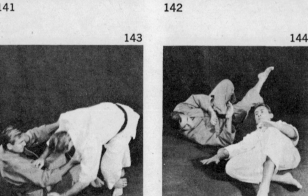

143. Using the downward pulling action of the arms, assisted by the pulling-down power of the body, throw is halfway executed.

144. As Receiver starts to go over, Thrower thrusts him with both hands and kicks upward with his right foot. After the thrust, Thrower releases hand grips.

Thrower must sit off *to the side* of Receiver, or Receiver will come straight down on top of him in that part of the action shown in photo 143. For safety, it is essential that Thrower release his hand grip in time to allow Receiver to fall properly or Receiver will be pulled down onto his head.

CIRCLE THROW

Begin in standard position.

145. Thrower steps in with his left foot.

146. Thrower places his right foot at Receiver's belt and pulls forward with both arms.

145

146

147

148

147. Thrower takes a hop on his left foot to place him in close to Receiver and sits down under him, continuing the arm movement. Receiver's balance should be completely broken at this point.

148. The throw is completed by thrusting action of both arms backward and over, aided by circular backward movement of the bent right leg. When Receiver is on the way over, Thrower must release his hand grips to allow Receiver to fall free.

Do not stiff-leg Receiver in that part of the action shown in photo 146 or he will come down on top of you. For safety, you must release your hand grips in time to let the Receiver fall properly, or he will come down on his head.

FREE-STYLE EXERCISE (randori)

In addition to demonstrating formal ability to execute the preceding throws and falls, the student must also demonstrate a working knowledge of contest procedures in order to advance to Green Belt.

Though he need not win points in contest, he should be able to engage in free-style practice properly, that is: throwing with opposition (rather than cooperation) from his Judo partner, blocking throws, applying counterthrows, etc.; using skill rather than force; exhibiting a comprehension of strategy; showing concern for his opponent's safety and, in general, conducting himself in a sportsmanlike manner. Violent, unnecessarily rough work and the application of illegal techniques disqualify a student from advancement. Finally, there is consideration of the student's general behavior and conduct while working toward his Green Belt degree.

Because Judo is such a close contact sport, good manners are essential to good play. Out of consideration for others in his group, each student is expected to treat the others courteously, to keep himself and his uniform clean, to work in a positive, cooperative way.

ADDITIONAL TRAINING

SALUTATION BOW AND THE COURTESY THROW

149. Most competitive sports have a form of salutation at the beginning and at the end of each match. Boxers touch gloves; fencers cross foils; wrestlers shake hands; Judo players bow.

Although I have eliminated much of the ceremonial bowing for Judo play, the bow at the beginning and end of each match or practice session is retained as a form of courteous salutation.

Another token of courtesy is shown to someone of higher belt rank when two players are practicing free-style; the lower-degree player allows the higher-degree player the first throw without opposition. This is simply a mark of respect—the privilege of rank being acknowledged. The courtesy throw does not apply in contest or tournament.

149

TIPS FOR TALL MEN

150.   Working with a shorter player, the tall man can grip at the back of opponent's belt and lift up, placing opponent in a very awkward position.

With his balance broken forward, the shorter opponent is easily thrown.

151.   When working with a short opponent who works in a low, squatting position, the tall man can grip opponent's pant leg and pull it up. This action makes him lose his balance and he can be thrown easily.

152.   Working with a shorter opponent, the tall man can break opponent's balance by gripping at the back of the collar and pulling up and forward.

153.   Working with a shorter player, the tall man can grip opponent's belt at the front and, by pulling up and forward, break opponent's balance.

TIPS FOR SHORT MEN

There are certain advantages which a short man has when playing Judo with a taller man. Naturally, he must be a *good* player in order to take advantage of the height relationship.

150   151

154. A good player can make it very difficult for a taller man to throw him, if he keeps his center of gravity behind himself and maintains low, squatting position. Shown here, the right-hand player finds it difficult to throw his shorter opponent.

155. Working with a taller opponent, the short man can very easily get into a position for the type of throw shown here.

152

153

154

155

156. Because of the arm reach of a tall man, it is ordinarily not advisable to attempt sacrificing throws if you are shorter; however, if your taller opponent works in a stance which places his upper body close to you and his legs are backed away, it is easy to apply sacrificing throws.

156

COUNTERS AGAINST STIFF-ARMING

Stiff-arming is the act of holding both arms out rigidly in an effort to prevent being thrown. It is a defensive technique which is used by inexperienced Judo players (mainly) and it results in very dull play. When a player stiff-arms, he may succeed in preventing being thrown, but he is at the same time in a very poor position to attempt throws himself. Try to avoid stiff-arming, even as a new player, for incorrect practices can easily become bad habits.

If you play with an opponent who uses stiff-arm tactics, the following counters will be very useful.

157. Player shown left is stiff-arming.

158. Player shown right takes advantage of the forward pushing movement of his opponent to apply a Lifting Sweeping Foot Throw.

Player at left has resisted with stiff-arming.

159, 160. Player shown right places his forearm into the crook of his opponent's elbow and forces it bent. This action not only releases the stiff arm, but forces opponent's body into an awkward stance, allowing the application of Back Straight Foot Throw (or similar throw).

157

158

159

160

161, 162. Player shown left stiff-arms. Right player reaches inside opponent's arm and reaches over to grab cloth high at the shoulder.

163. Pulling forward sharply, right player bends the stiff arm and applies Sweeping Foot Throw (or any similar throw).

161

162

163

164, 165. As player shown left stiff-arms, right player pushes up at the arms of his opponent and pulls them so that they slide over his shoulders. This allows him to move in close enough to apply a Spring Foot Throw (or similar throw).

166, 167. Left player stiff-arms. Right player grips opponent's belt and pulls sharply forward, allowing him to apply Upper Innercut (or similar) Throw.

164

165

166

167

168, 169. As left player stiff-arms, right player grips opponent at the back of his collar and pulls him forward into position for applying Spring Foot (or similar) Throw.

168   169

HOW TO BLOCK THROWS

Knowing how to throw properly is only one half of the knowledge necessary for Contest Judo or free-style practice; the other half is the knowledge of how to avoid being thrown by your opponent.

Beginning players should practice the following methods of blocking. These work in instances where the opponent is in the process of applying the throw. When you have had more practice, you will be able to proceed to the next stage. The more experience you have, the more easily you can "feel" or sense the beginning of a throwing attempt; you recognize a certain mode of shifting weight, of attempted positioning, etc., which tells you that your opponent is trying to set you up for a throw. The blocking action in this stage is evasive; you simply do not allow yourself to get set up for the throw.

In play between two Judo men who have relatively little experience, there is a great deal of action, many throws attempted, flurries of perceivable blocks, countertries, etc. As players become more sophisticated and sensitive, the play is more subtle. High-degree contests are characterized by relatively few actual throws; the two players are so responsive to "setups" that they spend most of their contest time in strategic planning rather than in haphazard and futile, energy-wasting activity.

The exact throw which is being attempted need not be defined. This block can be used whenever your opponent is in this backing-in position:

170.   As throw is attempted, right player places his hand at opponent's lower back (or hip) and pushes him away. This shifts his weight and makes the throw difficult to apply.

This block can be used in many different situations, whenever your opponent has his back toward you and attempts a throw:

171.   As throw is attempted, right player steps out from behind and uses arm action to bend opponent's body backward.

170   171

172.   As throw is attempted, right player uses arm action to push opponent to the left, off balance.

This block can be used whenever your opponent is in a position which is similar to the one shown:

173.   As right player attempts throw, left player uses arm action to push opponent to the side, off balance.

This type of block can be used against many different leg throws from the front:

174.   As left player attempts throw, right player blocks the throwing leg by pushing at it with his hand.

175.   As left player attempts Circle Throw (or any similar action), right player squats down low and pulls back.

TACTICAL USE OF THROWS FOR FREE-STYLE
PRACTICE AND CONTEST

In the same way that a game of chess is based upon your knowledge of the possible moves, the use of the throws in a tactical fashion must be based on a knowledge of the basic techniques of throwing. You need not be extremely skillful in your use of Judo to learn the tactics, but you will only have success in this phase of the training if you have a *strong working knowledge* of how to throw. There are many possible moves in Judo, as there are in chess. The more skilled you are as a player, the more combinations you can use, the more versatile you will be. As in chess, you can train yourself to be an aggressive player, a defensive player, or, best of all, a player who can plan strong attacks while anticipating and defending against threat of attack from the opposing player. In the following demonstrations, you will be shown a few examples of attack, response, counterattack. There could be many more parts for each series and in contest and free-style play you will use and encounter more sophisticated plans and responses. This material is intended to give you the *idea* of possible tactics. Only practice will give you ability to apply this idea.

Some examples of throwing, blocking and countering, using Green Belt throws:

172

173

174

175

176.   Player shown left attempts Sweeping Foot Throw.

177.   Player shown right evades the throw, using the cross body direction in which his foot is being pushed to pivot into position for body throw.

178.   Player shown right attempts Sweeping Foot Throw.

179.   Player shown left blocks by setting his foot into the mat and shifting his weight back, placing himself in position for right player's Kickback Throw.

176   177

178

179

180.   Player shown right attempts a body throw.

181.   Left player evades the attempted throw by stepping back and shifting his weight back.

182.   Right player uses new position of left player to apply Back Sweeping Foot Throw.

183.   Right player has attempted body throw which is being blocked by left player crouching.

180

181

182

183

184. Right player uses crouched position of left player to pivot in for Outercut Throw.

185. Right player attempts back leg throw which is evaded by left player shifting his weight forward

186. Right player takes advantage of forward motion to apply Lifting Sweeping Foot Throw.

187. Right player has attempted body throw, which left player blocks by buckling right player's knee with his knee, and shifting weight back.

184

185

186

187

188. Right player pivots on left foot and applies Inside Sweeping Foot Throw.

189. Right player attempts body throw.

190. Left player evades the throw by stepping back and stiff-arming.

191. Right player takes advantage of left player's awkward stance to apply Kneecap Throw.

188

189

190

191

THIRD-DEGREE BROWN BELT REQUIREMENTS AND TRAINING (sankyu)

THIRD BROWN BELT FALLS

11. Advanced Back Fall-Leaping
12. Advanced Side Fall
13. Advanced Side Fall—Leaping and Coming Up
14. Advanced Forward Fall—Leaping
15. Advanced Leaping Side Fall
16. Advanced Forward Leap

THIRD BROWN BELT THROWING (nage waza)

AND RECEIVING THROWS (ukemi)

1. Sweeping Foot Throw (de ashi harai)
2. Kneecap Throw (hiza guruma)
3. Sweeping Loin Throw (harai goshi)
4. Upper Innercut Throw (uchi mata)
5. Spring Foot Throw (hane goshi)
6. Innercut Throw (o-uchi gari)

COMBINATION THROWS (renrakuwaza)

1. Sweeping Foot—Straight Foot Throw
2. Sweeping Foot—Upper Innercut Throw
3. Straight Foot—Upper Innercut Throw
4. Straight Foot—Kickback Throw
5. Kneecap—Lateral Dash Throw

MAT TECHNIQUES (katame waza)—

HOLDING (osaekomi waza)

1. Side Shoulder Hold (kesagatame) and Three Variations
2. Crossbody Hold (yokoshihogatama) and Three Variations
3. Top Body Hold (kamishihogatama) and Three Variations

CONTEST—FREE-STYLE SPARRING (randori)

In addition to the demonstration of work done in the formal manner, listed above, you will now be required to win points in contest to achieve the rank of Third Brown Belt. In competition with other players of Green Belt rank, you must win against two different opponents.

For every advancement in degree, greater demands will be made upon you for technical perfection. It is not enough to learn additional techniques, you must learn to do them with more control, more grace, more dexterity. There should be an marked difference in the performance of form which you showed when working toward Green Belt and your work for Brown Belt; there should be improvements in your performance of forms as you advance to each higher degree.

Though not required for demonstration in the test, you should give serious attention to the instruction which follows the listed, required material. It is part of your continuing growth and development into a versatile Judo player.

Contest points are not required, of course, for those who are working for their degrees in forms alone. (See Introduction to Form Degrees, p. 57.)

ADDITIONAL TRAINING—MAT WORK

Basic Procedures
How to Evade Ground Work If You Are Thrown
How to Break Holds
    Escape from Side Shoulder Hold (3 Methods)
    Escape from Cross Body Hold (3 Methods)
    Escape from Top Body Hold (3 Methods)

ADDITIONAL TRAINING—CONTEST WORK

Preparation for Contest
Rules of Contest
Types of Contest
Use of Psychology in Contest

THIRD BROWN BELT FALLS

NUMBER ELEVEN FALL, ADVANCED BACK FALL—

LEAPING

Start from natural standing position.

D

192

193

194   195

192.   Squat.

193, 194.   Swing your arms backward; then spring up from the
balls of your feet as you swing your arms forward, thrusting hips
and legs up. Your entire body is off the mat and horizontal to the
ground.

195.   Ending position is exactly like #4 fall.

NUMBER TWELVE FALL, ADVANCED SIDE FALL

196. From a walking start, leading with the right foot, swing your right arm high, giving you momentum.

197. Tuck your head in; continue the swing of the arm, spring up from your right foot and vigorously twist yourself over.

198. Finish with side fall.

NUMBER THIRTEEN FALL, ADVANCED SIDE FALL— LEAPING AND COMING UP

199. This fall is exactly like #12 fall but is finished by allowing the momentum of the fall to continue and assist you in rising to a standing position at the end.

196

197

198

199

For training purposes, you may start to practice this fall by taking three steps, rather than one.

When beginning the practice of the advanced, leaping falls, it is helpful to work with a partner who can give you slight assistance. For instance, for the above falls, your partner could hold your right hand lifting slightly as you go over to keep you from falling too heavily. As you improve your ability, he may just hold his hand out to spot you. Eventually, with practice, you will be able to do the falls without help.

NUMBER FOURTEEN FALL, ADVANCED FORWARD

FALL—LEAPING

200.   As you take a step forward with your right foot, swing your arms up.

201, 202.   As you spring up from your right foot, fling your arms down and back and thrust your left leg up; your entire body leaving the mat as you turn over.

203.   Finish by hitting the mat with the bottoms of your feet (knees bent), arms slapping as your feet hit, your head off the mat. Your shoulders and the upper part of your back are on the mat at the finish of this fall, but your lower back does not touch the mat at all.

Begin practice of this fall by doing a handstand and falling over into the proper ending. You can tie a rope to the back of the belt and have two people hold it from the sides, giving firm support for beginning practice and giving less and less support as your ability increases.

NUMBER FIFTEEN FALL, ADVANCED LEAPING

SIDE FALL

204, 205.   Take a step to the side with your left foot as you swing your right arm and leg vigorously forward, then leap upward and twist your body over to your right.

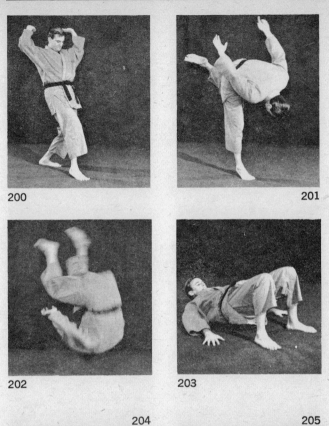

200

201

202

203

204

205

206.   The ending position is exactly like #9 fall. For training, you can add several steps in the beginning to give you needed momentum.

NUMBER SIXTEEN FALL, ADVANCED FORWARD LEAP

Begin from a relaxed standing position. Crouch slightly and swing your arms vigorously back.

207, 208.   Then as you leap up from the balls of your feet, swing your arms vigorously forward; straightening your legs when you are in the air.

209.   Ending position is the same as for #10 fall.

206

207

208

209

THIRD BROWN BELT THROWS
SWEEPING FOOT THROW

Standard beginning position.

210.   Thrower tilts Receiver toward Thrower's right with arm wheeling motion, shifting Receiver's weight onto his left foot.

211.   With the bottom of his left foot, Thrower catches Receiver's right instep.

212, 213.   As Thrower sweeps the foot out from under Receiver, Thrower reverses the arm wheeling motion, twisting Receiver

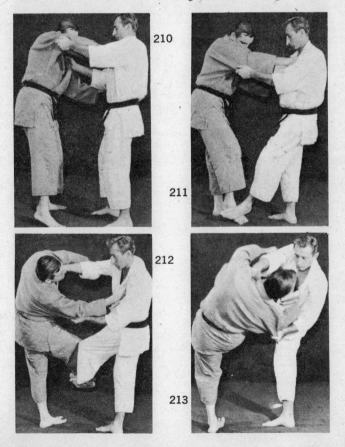

backward and down. As Receiver starts to fall, Thrower changes the direction of the circular pull by pulling Receiver toward him with his left hand and pushes down and around with his right arm.

Timing is the essential factor in this throw. The sweep is only effective when the Receiver is on one-point balance. For timing you can practice the sweep alone by walking with your training partner and fiinding the instant when the action must be done.

Sweeping Foot Throw is excellent because it is one of the few throws which can be done with equal ease from either right or left side and it can be executed whether your opponent is walking toward you or away from you. It combines with many other throws for very versatile contest use.

KNEECAP THROW

Standard beginning position.

214. Thrower sidesteps with his right foot, pointing his toe toward Receiver as he pulls Receiver in with both hands.

215. When Receiver's balance is broken, Thrower places bottom of his left foot directly underneath Receiver's kneecap, continuing the arm motion and twisting the body around in the direction of the throw.

216. Throw is completed by a sharply twisting arm movement as Thrower sweeps forcefully upward with his foot.

214

215

Thrower must keep the right leg slightly bent to get in proper position and the leg block must be done while Receiver is in one-point balance.

SWEEPING LOIN THROW

Begin in standard position.

217.   Use a *back-in pivot*, with feet very close together.

218.   As the pivot is completed, Receiver is pulled off balance. Thrower positions his right foot for sweep, as shown.

219.   Throw is executed with leg and arm movements made

216

217

218

219

simultaneously. The sweeping leg is swung up and back with the back of Thrower's thigh hitting the Receiver's thigh. Thrower's arms twist around to his left.

220.   The sweeping leg *carries through* as the arm motion continues for completion of the throw.

The *carrythrough* of the leg sweep is essential. Balance is maintained by the countermotion of leg and body. As the leg swings back, the body moves forward and around.

UPPER INNERCUT THROW

Standard beginning position.

221.   Thrower begins a *back-in pivot* as he starts to break Receiver's balance with wheeling arm movement.

222.   After completing the pivot, Thrower hits Receiver's upper inner thigh with the back of his right thigh, swinging his leg back and up with vigorous motion. As the leg sweeps, Thrower continues wheeling arm motion.

223.   The throw is completed by followthrough of the sweeping leg and continuation of the arm movement, assisted by twisting body motion.

With practice, this throw can be done to take the Receiver over in a high, spectacular throw by use of more and more sharply executed leg action.

SPRING FOOT THROW

The basic actions of Sweeping Loin Throw and Spring Foot Throw are the same. The variation is that the right leg is bent for the execution of the throw.

224.   *Back-in pivot.*

225.   Position bent leg for sweep, using arm motion simultaneously.

224

225

TRAINING ADVICE

Though the throw is demonstrated here against the one leg of Receiver, it can also be practiced against both legs. Proper execution of this throw demands more hip action than does the Sweeping Loin. 226

INNERCUT THROW

Standard beginning position.

227.   Thrower uses arm wheeling motion to tilt Receiver to Thrower's left as he hooks Receiver's left leg at the knee.

228.   Thrower holds captured leg firmly with his bent leg and starts twisting Receiver clockwise with arm and body motion.

229.   When Receiver begins to fall, Thrower allows the captured leg to fall free and completes the throw with vigorous arm and body movement.

Timing of the leg release is important. If it is released too soon, Receiver can regain his balance; if it is released too late, it interferes with safe fall of the Receiver and may result in Thrower being pulled down on the ground.

This throw, like Sweeping Foot Throw, can be done with equal ease on right or left sides and when players are moving in any direction.

228   229

COMBINATION THROWS

SWEEPING FOOT—STRAIGHT FOOT THROW

230.   Thrower attempts Sweeping Foot Throw, which is blocked, putting Receiver in vulnerable position for throw in opposite direction.

231.   Using to advantage the opposing pull of the Receiver, Thrower pivots on his left foot as he positions his right foot into place for Straight Foot Throw.

230   231

Reread Combination Throws before practicing any of the combinations. The training advice which is common to *all* combination throws is given there and will make it easier for you to follow the instruction.

The pivot is the essential part of the transition from Sweeping Foot to Straight Foot. Your balance and pivot exercises will help you do this properly and you are actually assisted in making the one-foot pivot by your opponent's resistance to the first throw attempt.

SWEEPING FOOT—UPPER INNERCUT THROW

232.   Thrower attempts Sweeping Foot Throw which is blocked, putting Receiver in position for throw in the opposite direction.

233.   Thrower pivots on his left foot into position for Upper Innercut Throw.

The situation here is similar to that shown in the previous combination. Thrower has chosen here to use Upper Innercut because Receiver's feet are spread apart.

STRAIGHT FOOT—UPPER INNERCUT THROW

234, 235.   Thrower attempts Straight Foot Throw, avoided by Receiver stepping over the straight foot. (Thrower failed to break Receiver's balance sufficiently.)

236. Upper Innercut can be executed without any change in position.

The transition from the attempted Straight Foot to the Upper Innercut is simply a matter of quick thinking and timing. This is an excellent combination.

STRAIGHT FOOT—KICKBACK THROW

237. Thrower attempts a Straight Foot Throw which is opposed by Receiver bending Thrower's knee (with his knee) and pulling back.

238, 239. Thrower pivots on the ball of his right foot and steps around with his left foot, placing himself in position to execute Kickback Throw.

Take advantage of the opposition of the Receiver to the first attempted throw and begin pushing him backward *as* you pivot into position. Since that is the direction in which he is already going, he is extremely vulnerable to being placed off balance.

KNEECAP—LATERAL DASH THROW

240. Thrower attempts Kneecap Throw, which is opposed by pulling to the opposite direction.

241, 242, 243. Using the opposing movement as an advantage, Thrower places his left foot down with toe pointing to Receiver so that he is in perfect position for Lateral Dash Throw.

Reversal of hand movement is, of course, required to make the throw.

MAT TECHNIQUE—HOLDING

Beginning students must very carefully reread Safety Rules for Judo Practice (p.20) and read Additional Training—Mat Work (p118). Improper methods of practice can result in unnecessary pain and possible injury which can be entirely avoided if instructions are followed. *INSTANT submission by tapping* is essential for safe practice of ground work. (In competition, a hold must be secured for 30 seconds to count for a full point.)

240

241

242

243

SIDE SHOULDER HOLD AND THREE VARIATIONS

(For simplicity in instructions, partner who executes the mat work is referred to as "you" or Thrower, and the Receiver may be referred to as "he.")

244

BASIC HOLD

244.   You sit in tight and close to Receiver on his right side. Put your right arm around his neck, placing right palm on mat. Your left hand grips cloth at his upper arm and you lock his right arm under your left arm. Your right knee is wedged into his right shoulder, your left leg extended back, bottom of left foot squarely on the mat, acting as a brace. Your head is held tightly into his body.

First Variation

245.   From the basic hold, Receiver has worked his right arm free. You pin his right arm with your left leg. Though you are not as well braced with your left leg in this position, you can apply pressure on the pinned arm with your leg, preventing his movement.

245

Second Variation

246.   From the basic hold, Receiver has worked his right arm free and holds it up. With your left hand push his right arm across his neck, lock it between your head and shoulder, regrip cloth at his shoulder with your left hand.

246

247

Third Variation

247. Receiver attempts to break basic hold by hooking your leg with his leg. His hooking attempt will ordinarily pull your upper body somewhat backward. As you are pulled back, slide your left arm over and around his right leg and grab your own pant legs high at the thighs. To apply pressure, press inward with your arms and straighten your legs.

CROSS BODY HOLD AND THREE VARIATIONS
BASIC HOLD

248. Working from the right side of Receiver, your body is across his; your left knee is wedged into his armpit, your right knee is wedged into his side (just above his hip); your left elbow is

248

locked into the left side of his neck, your right elbow is locked into his left side (just above the hip bone). Grip cloth with both hands. Hold your head down onto the mat.

First Variation

249.   From the basic Cross Body Hold, Receiver has attempted to use his left arm to push at your face. With your right hand, grip his wrist; with your left arm, reach under his arm and grip your own left wrist with your right hand. Locking pressure is applied by forcing down with your right hand as you lever up with your left arm.

Second Variation

250.   From the basic Cross Body Hold, Receiver attempts to roll you onto your head. To establish a counterweight, you straighten both legs and place your weight on your toes (as shown), and shift weight onto your elbows and onto his chest.

Third Variation

251.   From the basic hold, Receiver attempts to slide out from under. Reach under his head with your left arm and grip cloth at your own pant leg (at the thigh).

Cinch your elbows and knees *tightly* into Receiver. Each time he moves, tighten your locking action.

249

250

TOP BODY HOLD AND THREE VARIATIONS

BASIC HOLD

252. Place your body lengthwise over Receiver's body, your head pressed into his body (just above his belt). Your legs are drawn up, with weight on your knees and elbows. With both hands grip his belt at his sides, and lock your elbows into his sides.

First Variation

253. Same as basic hold, except that his arms are not pinned with your arms as in the basic hold.

Second Variation

254.   From basic hold, extend your legs and brace them onto the mat (on toes), spreading them to form a tripod with your upper body.

Third Variation

255.   Assume that with his left hand, he is attempting to pull you off. Slide your left hand under his upper arm and over his wrist. Pressure can be applied by pulling back with your left hand.

The basic hold gives a more secure hold, but you cannot always capture the arms as you go into this mat work. If you wish, you can apply a double wrist lock, locking both his wrists with both your hands, but it allows you more control if you lock with only one arm and keep the other free to control movement of his body.

254

255

ADDITIONAL TRAINING—MAT WORK
BASIC PROCEDURES

In Contest Judo you can get points for throwing techniques and for ground work, but you must be careful to let the throwing point be clearly demonstrated before you attempt ground work. If you

follow the Receiver down too quickly, it may be thought that you
have lost your balance and you will lose your throwing point. You
must allow a fraction of a second after your throw before you go
down onto the ground, though with some ground work you can
begin the technique while still standing. On the other hand, if you
hesitate for too long, Receiver will have an opportunity to cover
and protect himself and you will be unable to follow up with
ground work. Only experience and practice will show you how to
gain the ground work point without risking the loss of the throwing point.

256, 257.   Receiver has clearly been thrown for a point; without
losing your balance forward, start to slide your arm around into
position for mat hold; take hold.

256

257

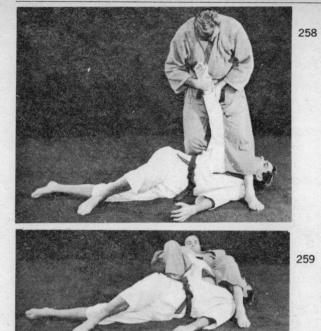

258, 259. Receiver has clearly been thrown. As soon as he hits the mat, take the step over; apply arm lock.

260, 261. Receiver has clearly been thrown: without losing your balance forward, maintain grip on lapels and apply choke as soon as he is on the ground.

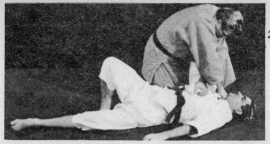

261

The above are simply examples of different types of mat work to show you the general positioning and body movements from throw to mat. Actual mat-work techniques will be taught as you go on.

HOW TO EVADE GROUND WORK IF YOU ARE THROWN

262, 263. You have been thrown. Before Thrower can attempt

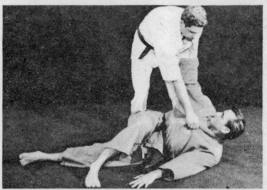

262

263

ground work, draw your knee up toward your head and cover your head with your arms.

264.   After being thrown, roll over, brace and spread your legs; grip the back of your collar with both hands; flatten yourself onto the mat.

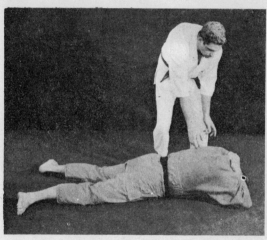

264

265, 266, 267.   After being thrown, roll in the direction away from Thrower rolling over twice to place you clear of him, get up.

HOW TO BREAK HOLDS: ESCAPE FROM
SIDE SHOULDER HOLD (3 METHODS)

You are captured in Side Shoulder Hold.

265

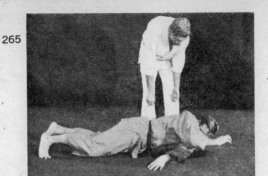

266

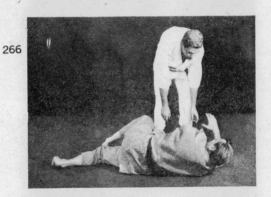

267

268

269

270

271

First Method

268, 269. With your right hand, push up and back at Thrower's left knee.

270. With your left heel, hook his knee, as shown.

271. To escape, pull his leg with your left leg; with your left hand grab cloth at his left shoulder and pull sharply; with your right hand grip cloth at his chest and push. While you are doing these arm and leg movements, your entire body is rolling him over you.

Second Method

272. Throw your body and legs to the left side.

273, 274. From the position in photo 272, fling your legs and body to the right, twisting your body as you go over and sharply drawing your right arm under you. You may have to repeat this several times to effect escape.

275

276

277

Third Method

275.   With both your hands, grip his belt at the back and bridge your body upward as you jerk up on his belt, getting his hip off the mat.

276.   When his hip is off the mat, slide your right knee under his hip.

277.   Effect escape by rolling to the left as you raise him with your knee and pull him over you with both arms.

HOW TO BREAK HOLDS: ESCAPE FROM CROSS BODY HOLD (3 METHODS)

278.   Thrower has taken Cross Body Hold on you.

First Method

279.   With your left hand grip back of his jacket; with your right hand grip his belt; at the same time, brace your feet and push him with your body and arms toward your right.

280.   His reaction to your pushing action will be to oppose it; using his opposing action to aid you, reverse the action in photo 279 and pull him over you with your arms, rolling with your body, also.

278

279

280

Second Method

281.   With your left hand grip back of his jacket and pull him toward your left (using body motion to assist); with your right hand push his left foot, removing part of his bracing strength.

282.   His reaction will be to oppose your action by pulling back. Using his reaction to aid you, jerk your body to the right as you push with your left hand. With your right hand, keep his left leg locked. Your braced leg will help you bridge your body as you twist to the right.

Third Method

283.   With your right hand, grip his belt at the back and with your left hand grip cloth at his lapel. Using a snappy motion, push him toward your feet with both hands.

281

282

283

284.   His reaction will be to resist on the opposite direction. Using his action to assist you, pull sharply back with both hands (using body motion, as well) to roll him over your head.

HOW TO BREAK HOLDS: ESCAPE FROM TOP BODY HOLD (3 METHODS)

285.   Thrower has effected Top Body Hold.

First Method

286.   With both hands, grip his belt at the back as you swing your legs in a whipping action to the right side.

287.   As he resists your action, use his reaction to help you in the next step. Whip your legs over toward the left as you twist him with your arms.

288.   A successful escape using this method will allow you to take Top Body Hold on him.

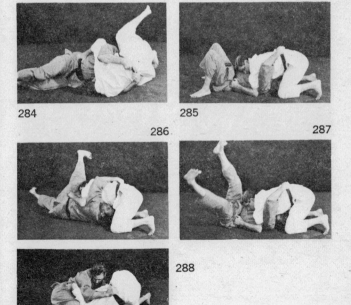

284

285

286

287

288

289

290

291

292

Second Method

289. Bracing your feet on the mat (knees bent as shown), arch your body upward as you pull up on him with both hands gripping the back of his belt.

290. Thrust him backward with your hands as you drop down and slide forward.

Third Method

291. Swing your legs sharply over and place them at a 90° angle to his body, as you pull up with both your hands at the back of his belt.

292. Repeat the swinging leg movement once or twice and complete escape by rolling over onto your side.

ADDITIONAL TRAINING—CONTEST WORK

As for any sport, training for Contest Judo requires more time, devotion, energy and firmness of purpose than does play for fun or exercise. In addition to working on Judo techniques to perfection, you must be in top physical and mental health. Follow a sensible regime of diet and sleep. Daily roadwork and exercise will bring your body to the peak of efficiency.

It is just as important to be mentally alert as it is to be physically fit. If you are distracted by worry, fear, anger or any emotional upset, you will be working against heavy odds, no matter how much Judo you know. Before contest, consciously develop an attitude of calm. Practice putting all distracting or negative thoughts out of your mind and concentrate on the *idea* of Judo, concentrate on mental images of Judo play, concentrate on the will to do your best.

RULES OF CONTEST

Rules of Sport Judo contest are fairly well established all over the world. Here is a general set of rules which can be adapted to most Judo contests. Differences from place to place are minor with one important exception—the AAU rules include weight classes. As world participation in Sport Judo increases, there may be changes in the rules to accommodate new situations. Perhaps the weight class will be used for international tournament—or perhaps there will be a new way of competing based on a combination of proficiency (belt rank) and weight class. Such a method seems to me to be most desirable because it matches players of nearly equal skill and equal weight. The traditional system of play goes on the assumption that weight plays no part in contest. (It was not a problem when the players were almost all small men.) But weight *does* have importance in Judo play and it has been seen in international contest that between two men of equal skill, the big man has a definite advantage over the small man.

Before entering any contest, the players should know what is required of entrants; who is allowed to compete; what is the procedure for entering contest; special rules of the contest, etc. All this information should be given *in writing* well in advance of the contest date.

At the beginning of the tournament, major points of the contest rules should be given in the hearing of all contestants, judges and referees.

Contest Area: Judo competition is held on a mat or padded surface about 30′ x 30′. The mat may be between two and three inches in thickness. Any material which is ordinarily practical for a gym mat is suitable. Matting should be covered with a canvas or vinyl cover. Japanese straw mats may be used.

Uniform: The standard Judo uniform should be worn. If the imported uniforms are not available, a domestic copy may be improvised which follows the same pattern and allows freedom of movement.

Referee: The referee ordinarily makes the final decision in a match. Normally, there are one or two judges with whom the referee will consult if he is in doubt about a point. (In minor contests it is permissible to have only a referee. In major tournaments it is the practice to have one or two judges as well.) Sometimes the rules will permit the judges to dispute the decision of the referee and outvote him. The referee is the only person except the contestants who is allowed on the mat during the match. The judges are placed at opposite sides of the mat and at its edge.

Timekeeper and Secretary: A timekeeper should have only the duty of keeping time on each match and there should be a secretary who records the outcome of each match.

Contestant Degrees and Weight: Contestants should be matched according to the rules of the contest. Where proficiency ratings alone are used, all contestants must be matched with opponents of equal rank. If a contestant wears a belt of a lower degree than he actually holds, it is an infraction of the rules and calls for immediate disqualification. Where the contest rules require weight classes, there should be a weighing-in on the same day that the contest is held.

Start and Finish of a Match: At a signal from the referee, the contestants approach each other, standing about 12 feet apart. They bow. The bow is the formal salutation which precedes and ends every match. When the referee signals that a match is finished, the contestants return to the starting point and bow.

Signal to start the match is given by the timekeeper. The match is ended at a signal from the timekeeper when the time is up, or when the referee signals that a match is over.

Time is usually three minutes for a match in the lower-degree contests and usually five minutes for each match in the higher degrees. The referee may extend a match to break a tie.

Timeout is allowed if a player must adjust his uniform, if there is a minor injury, or if there is any question of scoring which needs to be decided. If the referee wishes to examine a contestant to determine fitness to contine, he calls timeout. A contestant indicates that he wishes timeout by backing away from his opponent and dropping down on one knee. The referee may call timeout for any reason. A contestant may not ask for timeout more than three times in any one match.

Fitness: Contestants must take responsibility for being in good health and fit to compete. If there is any question about fitness, a doctor should be seen. The contestants must take responsibility for any injury incurred during a match. Each contestant is responsible for declaring an injury if it is not seen by the referee.

Contestants must have fingernails and toenails cut short and smooth. Avoid body and breath ordor. Contestants may not wear rings, ornaments, medals or any other objects which might cause injury to the opponent.

Points: Points are called by the referee. Decisions on points are made by the referee and judges.

Full points are made by: (1) completing a throw with full control of the opponent and without loss of balance; (2) use of a Judo choke which forces the opponent to submit; (3) use of Arm or Leg Lock which restrains the opponent for 30 seconds; (4) use of Judo hold which restrains the opponent for 30 seconds.

Half points are made if: (1) a throw is completed fully, but the form is less than perfect; (2) a hold or lock is maintained for 25 seconds.

Mat-work points are valid when: (1) the hold or lock is started as standing work and the opponent is taken down while hold or lock is maintained; (2) the hold or lock is taken while opponent is on the ground as the result of an imperfect throw or his own loss of balance; (3) a poorly executed throw has put contestant A on the ground and contestant B attempts mat work; contestant A is allowed to counter with mat work and gains a point if he is successful.

Judo choking techniques are generally permitted, though there is now a tendency away from chokes for contest play.

Points by Submission and Default: A point is gained if the opponent submits to a choke, lock or hold. The usual signal for submission is by tapping twice. If the opponent fails to submit, but the referee sees that the hold, lock or choke is firmly taken and, in his opinion, is a good point, he may terminate the match before 30 seconds.

Winning by default is allowed under some circumstances. My opinion is that a match should be won on the basis of a contestant's superior skill, rather than on the basis of his opponent's inadequacy. However, it is fairly common to award a match to an injured contestant even when the injury is through no clear fault of either contestant, or to award a match to the opponent of a contestant who violates a rule.

Any technique applied off the mat area is not allowed. To count for a point, at least half the opponent's body must remain on the mat at the completion of a throw. In mat work, both contestants must have at least half their bodies on the mat at the time a mat work technique is applied.

Illegal Techniques: None of the following techniques are allowed in Judo contest. Any contestant who uses them is disqualified.

1. Applying leg scissors against head, neck or stomach.

2. Applying holding or locking techniques which could result in serious injury.

3. Dragging an opponent to the ground without attempting a standard Judo throw.

4. Choking against the windpipe.

5. Falling onto opponent with body, knee or arm.

6. Biting, scratching, pinching, gouging, bending fingers back or any other act which falls outside of standard Judo practice and which is intended to cause pain, such as kicking into the shin or a knee into the groin.

TYPES OF CONTEST

One-Point Contest: This is the most common form of contest. Individual players are matched according to previously decided classes: by belt rank, by weight, or by belt rank and weight. Whichever contestant wins a full point is the winner of that match. The advantage of single-point contest is that it allows large numbers of players to compete in one tournament. In playoffs, the one-point system is used almost exclusively. The disadvantages of single-point contest are: It does not allow for the use of full range of technique, including mat work. It does not show the players in true form; when only one point is required, it can be made on a lucky throw.

Two Out of Three Points: Contestants are matched in the same manner as above, according to classes previously determined. The player who gets two full points is the winner. Matches are longer in this type of play, and fewer contestants can participate, but it is the best form of contest for showing full range of technique. This is the method of contest which should be used for degree advancement. (See requirements for the degrees.)

Team Play: The two kinds of team play are elimination and point accumulation.

Elimination: A single player stays in the match as long as he defeats players from the opposing team. When he is defeated, the winner from the other team plays as many men as he can defeat. The team which first has all its men defeated is the losing team. The disadvantage of this method is that it often does not demonstrate the skill of the entire team and leads to a "star" system of training, where one player is groomed and the others more or less neglected.

Point Accumulation: The type of play which best measures the ability of all team members, matches every player of one team against a player from the opposing team. For instance, the two teams draw numbers and the two players who draw "#1" compete, the two players who draw "#2" compete, etc. The team with the highest total number of points is the winner.

USE OF PSYCHOLOGY IN CONTEST

As you become more and more proficient in Judo play, you will learn how to manipulate your opponent psychologically as well as physically. There are a number of ways in which this works:

1. Unconsciously, as you become a better player, the confidence you have in yourself shows to your opponent. Without making any visible effort, your assurance is apparent.

2. Deliberately cultivate the outward mannerisms of confidence and you will see that your opponent will react differently to you than if you give him signals that tell him you are not sure of yourself or of your ability. Even if you *feel* outclassed, don't show it. Avoid making the facial expressions which indicate fear, apology or fatigue.

3. No matter how important the contest is and what is at stake—degree promotion, trophy or the honor of your team—you must not allow yourself to become angry with an opponent. Anger consumes energy and interferes with your ability to plan sensibly. If you encounter an angry opponent, do not react to him, unless it is to smile. An angry opponent is already at a disadvantage and if you appear calm and pleasant, if will further upset his equilibrium.

SECOND-DEGREE BROWN BELT REQUIREMENTS (nikyu)

SECOND BROWN BELT THROWING (nage waza)
AND RECEIVING THROWS (ukemi)

1. Lifting Sweeping Foot Throw (harai tsurikomi ashi)
2. Inside Sweeping Foot Throw (ko uchi gari)
3. Back Sweeping Foot Throw (ko soto gari)
4. Outercut Throw (ko soto gake)
5. Pulling-down Straight Foot Throw (uki otoshi)
6. Side Sweeping Foot Throw (okuri ashi harai)

COMBINATION THROWS (renraku waza)

1. Lifting Sweeping Foot—Outercut Throw
2. Back Sweeping Foot—Kickback Throw
3. Outercut—Inside Sweeping Foot Throw
4. Inside Sweeping Foot—Pulling-down Straight Foot Throw
5. Sweeping Foot—Sweeping Loin Throw
6. Spring Foot—Outercut Throw

MAT TECHNIQUES (katame waza)—
HOLDING (osaekomi waza)

1. Reverse Side Shoulder Hold (ushiro kesagatame)
2. Arm and Head Shoulder Hold (makura kesagatame)
3. Kneeling Side Shoulder Hold (katagatame)
4. Straddling Body Hold (tateshihogatame)

MAT TECHNIQUES—CHOKES (shime waza)

1. Cross Arm, Palms Down Choke (namijuji jime)
2. Front Sliding Choke (tsukikomi-jime)
3. Rear Bar Choke (katahu jime)
4. Knuckle Choke (ryote jime)
5. One-Arm Cross Choke (katajuji jime)

MAT TECHNIQUES—ARM LOCKS (kansetsu waza)

1. Bent Arm Lock—In (ude garami)
2. Straight Arm Lock—Out with Arm Pressure (ude gatame)
3. Straight Arm Lock—Up with Leg Pressure (ude gatame)
4. Straight Arm Lock with Hip Pressure (ude-hishigi-juji-gatame)
5. Combination Straight Arm Lock into Bent Arm Lock (ude-gatame ude-garami)

CONTEST (randori)

In addition to excellent performance of the techniques listed above (in the formal manner) you will be required to win points in contest, working against two opponents of Third-Degree Brown Belt.

ADDITIONAL TRAINING—NOT REQUIRED FOR TEST

Releases from Chokes and Locks

SECOND BROWN BELT THROWS
LIFTING SWEEPING FOOT THROW

293. Players start in standard beginning position; Thrower shown facing rear.

294. Thrower sidesteps with his right foot, pointing it at a 45° angle toward Receiver and begins to pull Receiver forward and up onto his toes. As Receiver is being pulled, Thrower places his left foot at Receiver's ankle.

295. Thrower completes throw by pulling Receiver into his chest; then shifting the direction of the arm movement to twist around and down while following through with the foot sweep.

INSIDE SWEEPING FOOT THROW

296. Thrower shifts weight of Receiver so that he is balanced onto his left foot.

297. With the bottom of his right foot, Thrower sweeps Receiver's right foot (at the ankle) outward and forward.

298. Throw is completed by arm movement as the swept foot is brought up high. Thrower's left hand pulls toward himself, then down and around as his right hand pushes down and around.

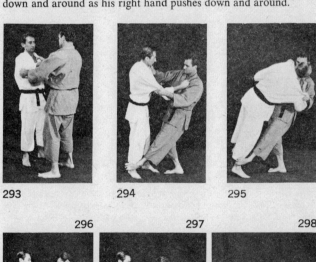

293   294   295

296   297   298

BACK SWEEPING FOOT THROW

Timing and action of this throw are similar to basic Sweeping Foot; relative positioning of Thrower and Receiver are shifted.

299.   From starting position, facing Receiver, Thrower steps behind himself with his right foot so that he is at a 45° angle to Receiver.

300.   With the bottom of his left foot, Thrower sweeps Receiver's right foot at the heel; beginning the around and down circular movement with his arms when Receiver's balance is well broken.

301.   Bringing the swept foot up high, Thrower completes throw by continuing the circular arm movement with vigor.

OUTERCUT THROW

302.   As Receiver is tilted backward (or as he moves himself back), Thrower hooks his leg around from the outside, catching Receiver's knee. In this sequence, Thrower catches the right leg with his left leg; the leg to be caught is the one which is moving.
303.   Clamping the captured leg and bringing it forward, Thrower begins to cant Receiver's body around.

304.   Throw is completed by locking the captured leg firmly and pulling it forward as the down-and-around arm movement is vigorously executed.

This throw can be done with equal ease on either side. Balancing exercises (which help you maintain good strong position on one leg) will assist you in skillful use of the throw.

PULLING-DOWN STRAIGHT FOOT THROW

305.   As Thrower pulls down on Receiver, he bends his left leg behind him.

306.   Continuing the downward pull on Receiver, Thrower places his bent leg on the mat.

307.   As he extends his right foot, placing it ankle-to-ankle at Receiver's right foot, Thrower continues downward pull, adding circular motion.

299

300

301

302

303

304

305

306

307

308. Throw is completed by continuing the pull down and around.

TRAINING ADVICE

Keep the toes of the left foot extended so that weight is on the instep of the foot (rather than on the toes). The right leg is held firm and straight, with the ball of the foot planted strongly on the mat. For beginning practice, go down onto the knee slowly. With practice you can eliminate the intermediate step shown in photo 306.

SIDE SWEEPING FOOT THROW

The timing and major action of this throw are similar to Sweeping Foot Throw.

309. Thrower tilts Receiver so that most of his weight is on his left foot.

310. With his left foot, Thrower sweeps raised foot of Receiver.

311. As the raised foot is swept, Thrower reverses tilting motion to shift Receiver's weight toward the swept foot.

312. Sweep is completed, taking both feet of the Receiver. At the finish, Thrower twists Receiver around and down.

Avoid pulling down on the Receiver. As the tilt is made, pull up. Only at the finish should the downward pull be made.

COMBINATION THROWS
LIFTING SWEEPING FOOT—OUTERCUT THROW

313. Thrower attempts Lifting Sweeping Foot Throw which Receiver resists by pulling himself back.

314. Taking advantage of Receiver's backward movement, Thrower executes Outercut Throw.

BACK SWEEPING FOOT—KICKBACK THROW

315. Thrower attempts Back Sweeping Foot Throw, which is unsuccessful because Receiver is not off balance.

316. Thrower steps in for Kickback Throw.

308

309

310

311

312

313

314

315

316

OUTERCUT—INSIDE SWEEPING FOOT THROW

317.   Thrower attempts Outercut, which is unsuccessful (either because he has not completely captured Receiver's leg or has not adequately broken Receiver's balance with proper arm movement).

318.   Taking advantage of Receiver's leg in forward position, Thrower executes Inside Sweeping Foot Throw.

INSIDE SWEEPING FOOT—PULLING-DOWN STRAIGHT FOOT THROW

319.   Thrower attempts Inside Sweeping Foot Throw which is not properly timed.

320, 321.   Pivoting on the ball of his left foot, Thrower swings his right leg out and drops down into position for Pulling-down Straight Foot Throw.

SWEEPING FOOT—SWEEPING LOIN THROW

322.   Thrower attempts Sweeping Foot Throw which is not successful.

323.   He executes Sweeping Loin Throw. In the transition from the first throw attempted and the second throw executed, Thrower does not put his right foot down, but pivots on the ball of his left foot to get into correct position.

SPRING FOOT—OUTERCUT THROW

324.   Thrower attempts Spring Foot Throw which Receiver opposes by pulling back.

325.   Thrower is pulled onto his right foot and uses Receiver's backward motion to assist him in executing Outercut Throw with his left leg.

317

318

319

320

321

322

323

324

325

326   327

MAT TECHNIQUES—HOLDING
REVERSE SIDE SHOULDER HOLD

326.   Sitting on your right hip, lock your right knee firmly into
his side; the bottom of your left foot is braced onto the mat, but
moveable in the event he tries to escape; your right arm is under
his neck and grasps cloth at his shoulder; your left hand grips his
belt at his right side; maintain hold by wedging him into your right
leg with your arms; press your upper body onto his chest to prevent
escape.

327.   Same hold from different view.

ARM AND HEAD SHOULDER HOLD

328.   Sitting on your right hip, your right leg is wedged under his
right shoulder; left foot is braced on the mat; upper part of your
body lies across his chest; right arm is locked into his left side; right
hand grips cloth at his left shoulder; left arm is locked at the left
side of his head and grips cloth under his left shoulder; hold head
down; squeeze your body into his chest, and lock him between
your right leg and your arms.

329.   Same hold, different view.

KNEELING SIDE SHOULDER HOLD

330.   Kneeling on your right knee, place it at his right side; left
leg is extended with foot braced on the mat; right arm is around
his neck, gripping cloth at his right shoulder; your head and
shoulder are braced into his head, neck and shoulder; left hand
grips cloth at his right upper arm; maintain hold by clamping him
between your right arm and right knee with the left foot acting as
a brace.

STRADDLING BODY HOLD

331. Kneeling, your knees are at the sides of his hips, braced on your toes; your arms are under his arms, gripping cloth on the upper shoulders; your chest is on his chest; your head is placed beside his head. Hold is maintained by pulling toward you with your arms and squeezing in with your knees.

MAT TECHNIQUES—CHOKES

Before beginning the practice of *any* chokes, reread carefully the section on Safety Rules for Judo Practice (p. 20). Courtesy and safety demand that you practice chokes properly. Do not work with partners who fail to observe the safety rules. It is not brave, it is *foolish* not to tap for release as soon as a choke is applied.

CROSS ARM, PALMS DOWN CHOKE

Before starting the practice of chokes, reread *carefully* the section on Safety Rules for Judo Practice (p. 20). Improper methods of practice can result in unnecessary pain or injury. Particularly avoid choking across the windpipe as windpipe chokes can be very dangerous. (Most contest rules do not allow use of windpipe chokes.)

Most chokes can be applied from standing, seated, kneeling or straddling position (as shown).

328

329

330

331

332. With crossed hands, grip high at the collar; thumbs inside the cloth, palms down. Pull toward you with a small, jerky movement and apply pressure against the side of neck with your forearms. Release pressure *instantly* upon tapping signal.

FRONT SLIDING CHOKE

333. With your right hand grip both his lapels in one hand, your forefinger between the lapels; with your left hand grip his left lapel just below your right hand; apply pressure by pulling down with your left hand as you slide your right hand up without releasing your grip on the jacket; it is his own jacket which chokes him.

REAR BAR CHOKE

334. This choke can only be applied when you are in back of your opponent. In tournament, it might be applied if he attempts a throw which places him in front of you.

With your right hand, grip cloth at his left shoulder or lapel, natural grip; place your left forearm at the right side of his neck. Apply pressure by pressing against his neck with your forearm as you pull toward you with your right hand.

KNUCKLE CHOKE

335. With your arms held straight, grip cloth at the sides of his neck with your fingers inside the cloth, thumb outside (unnatural grip). Give slight jerky motion forward to take up slack in his jacket. Apply pressure by turning your fists outward so that your two large knuckles grind into sides of his neck.

Release pressure *instantly* upon tapping signal.

ONE-ARM CROSS CHOKE

336. With your right hand, reach cross body and grip cloth high at his right collar, unnatural grip; left hand grips cloth at his chest level.

Pressure is applied by levering back against the side of his neck with your right forearm as you pull across with your left arm.

MAT TECHNIQUES—ARM LOCKS
BENT ARM LOCK—IN

337. Thrower has Receiver on the mat, seated on Receiver's left side, with your left elbow locked into his neck and shoulder, left hand gripping his left wrist with unnatural grip. With your right hand reach under Receiver's left arm and grip your own left wrist. Lock is maintained by cinching his captured arm tightly into your body as you lean into his arm.

332

333

334

335

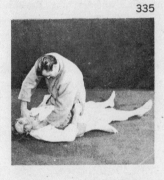

336

337

STRAIGHT ARM LOCK—OUT WITH ARM PRESSURE

338.   Thrower is seated at Receiver's left side. With your left arm, reach over Receiver's left arm (at the elbow) and grip your right wrist. Your right hand grips his left wrist. This lock is most effective if Receiver's arm is extended. Pressure is applied by levering down on his wrist with your right hand, leaning back with your body into his body, raising up on his elbow with your left forearm.

STRAIGHT ARM LOCK—UP WITH LEG PRESSURE

339.   Thrower has Receiver on the mat, face down. Kneel on your right knee at Receiver's right side. With both your hands, grip his right wrist, holding his arm straight, palm up. Your left leg is over his captured arm, with the inside of the thigh placed at his elbow. The left leg is kept straight and wedged into the mat for balance and leverage. Pressure is applied by pulling up on his captured arm.

STRAIGHT ARM LOCK—WITH HIP PRESSURE

340.   After effecting throw, you grip Receiver's right wrist with both your hands, keeping his captured arm extended straight. Step across his neck with your left foot, lower yourself onto the mat on your back, placing your hip close to his right shoulder; top of your right foot is wedged into Receiver's right side. Pressure is applied by levering his elbow against either of your thighs as you raise your hips.

COMBINATION STRAIGHT ARM LOCK INTO BENT ARM LOCK

341.   Thrower has Receiver on the mat. From the throw, lower yourself onto your right knee as you capture Receiver's right arm under your left armpit and slide your left arm around the captured arm. Your left forearm is locked under Receiver's right elbow; your right hand is placed at his right shoulder; with your left hand grip your own right wrist. Pressure is applied by pushing down at the shoulder with the right hand and raising up against the captured elbow with the left forearm; additional leverage can be had by leaning your upper body back. This lock can only be effective if Receiver's arm is extended with the palm up.

342.   If Receiver's arm is bent, the lock is taken in the same manner, but pressure is applied by levering up and *outward* against the captured elbow.

ADDITIONAL TRAINING

RELEASES FROM CHOKES AND LOCKS

The two best releases from front chokes are:

1. With the palms of your hands, press inward at your opponent's elbows. This is the weakest area of his arms and relatively little pressure will effect release.

2. Clasp your hands together *through* his arms and lever upward against his elbow with your forearm.

Arm locks can sometimes be broken in the following manner: First, grip cloth at your captured arm and oppose the direction of the push (or pull) to relieve pressure. Then, turn you arm over and bend it. If you are able to turn and bend, you should be able to escape.

If your opponent has applied a choke or hold with proper technique, you may not be able to effect release before the time allowed. If there is any weakness in his technique; if he has applied a sloppy choke or hold, the above escape methods can work.

338

339

340

341

342

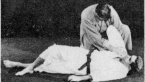

FIRST-DEGREE BROWN BELT REQUIREMENTS (ikkyu)
FIRST BROWN BELT THROWING (nage waza)

1. Rear Hip Throw (ushiro goshi)
2. Reverse Hip Throw (utsuri goshi)
3. Binding Throw (soto makikomi)
4. Shouldering Throw (katahuruma)
5. Crab Claw Throw (kamiwaza)
6. Inside Lateral Dash Throw (sumigaeshi)

COMBINATION THROWS (renraku waza)

1. Back Sweeping Foot—Rear Hip Throw
2. Circle—Inside Lateral Dash Throw
3. Binding—Pulling-down Straight Foot Throw
4. Pulling-down Straight Foot—Crab Claw Throw
5. Inside Sweeping Foot—Shouldering Throw
6. Spring Foot—Outercut Throw

MAT TECHNIQUES (katame waza)—
CHOKES (shime waza)

1. Rear Sliding Choke (okurieri jime)
2. Rear Lapel Choke (sode guruma jime)
3. Under and Over Arm Choke (kataha jime)
4. Rear Bare Body Choke (hadaka jime)
5. Loop Choke (kata juji jime)

MAT TECHNIQUES—ARM LOCKS (kansetsu waza)
AND ANKLE LOCK

1. Straight Arm Lock with Body Lever (taigatame udekujiki)
2. Straight Arm Lock with Leg Lever (hizagatame udekujiki)
3. Straight Arm Lock into Body (haragatame udekujiki)
4. Rear Bent Arm Lock (ude garami)
5. Ankle Lock (ashikujiki)

CONTEST (randori)

In addition to the excellent performance of the techniques listed above (done in the formal manner) you must win points in contest against two Second-Degree Brown Belt opponents.

FIRST BROWN BELT THROWS
REAR HIP THROW

343. Players start from standard throwing practice position Receiver shown right.

344. *Receiver* attempts body throw, stepping across with his right foot.

345. Thrower blocks the attempted body throw by pulling back, squatting and bending Receiver's knees or pressing with his hand at Receiver's hip.

346. Thrower squats so that his thighs are lower than Receiver's hips and pulls Receiver back off balance.

347. Throw is effected by combination of pulling back on Receiver's upper body, straightening your body to lift him off the ground and bouncing his lower body forward and up.

REVERSE HIP THROW

348. From standard starting position, Thrower, shown right, steps in deep with left foot.

343

344

345

346

347

348

349.   As you step behind Receiver with your right foot, bend Receiver backward to break his balance; bend your knees as shown, lean your upper body left, placing your hips just below his hips.

350.   Throw is completed by pulling him around and down with your arms and twisting your body sharply to follow the around and downward motion.

BINDING THROW

351.   From standard beginning stance, Thrower, shown right, pivots on the ball of left foot, turns body and starts pulling Receiver's right arm forward.

352.   With your right foot step around (moving counterclockwise) so that your back faces Receiver's right side. As you turn, pull his right arm with your left hand, release your right hand grip and bring your right arm over his arm.

353.   Throw is effected by using body weight to take Receiver down; you raise your right leg and lower yourself to the mat.

354.   Ending position as shown; your own fall is taken with your hip and forearm on the mat.

Avoid falling backward onto Receiver, you could hurt his ribs. Some styles of Judo do not allow this throw in contest. Because body weight is so important, this throw can be done by a larger man on a smaller man, but is quite impractical for a small man against a big man.

SHOULDERING THROW

355.   From standard beginning position, Thrower, shown right, breaks Receiver's balance forward sharply.

356.   With your right foot, step in between Receiver's feet; keeping upper body erect, squat as shown; your right hand grips cloth at the back of his right leg, as your left hand pulls him across your shoulders.

357.   Throw is executed by toppling him across your shoulders

349

350

351

352

353

354

355

356

357

in a seesaw motion; your left hand pulls as your right hand lifts and pushes over. The throw can be accelerated by springing up with your body as Receiver is going over.

CRAB CLAW THROW

358. From standard beginning position, Thrower, shown left, steps around, placing right foot in back of left foot.

359. Releasing right-hand grip, start to place right hand on the mat as you bring your left leg up in front of Receiver.

360. When your right hand is on the mat, spring up from your right foot and clasp your legs around Receiver's body. Ideally, your left leg is at his upper thighs and your right leg is just above his knees.

361. Throw is completed by jerking back sharply with your left hand, twisting your body and legs back so that you fall on your back. The combined arm, legs and body action will take him to the mat.

This throw is not always allowed in contest because of the possibility of leg injury.

INSIDE LATERAL DASH THROW

362. Beginning action is the same as for the basic Lateral Dash Throw.

363, 364. As the throw is being executed, place your right instep at Receiver's lower leg, and complete the throw with your feet raising his legs as he goes over.

COMBINATION THROWS

BACK SWEEPING FOOT—REAR HIP THROW

365. Thrower attempts Back Sweeping Foot Throw which is opposed by Receiver.

366. Thrower steps onto his left foot and steps into position for Rear Hip Throw.

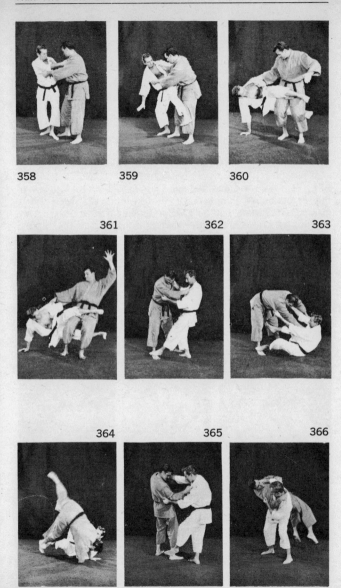

358

359

360

361

362

363

364

365

366

CIRCLE—INSIDE LATERAL DASH THROW

367. Thrower attempts Circle Throw, which Receiver opposes by squatting.

368, 369. Thrower places his right foot down and takes advantage of squatting and forward movement of Receiver to execute Inside Lateral Dash Throw.

BINDING—PULLING-DOWN STRAIGHT FOOT THROW

370. Thrower attempts Binding Throw which is opposed.

371. Thrower executes Pulling-down Straight Foot Throw. In this execution of Pulling-down Straight Foot, Thrower simply maintains the same grip he had for Binding Throw, drops down onto his left knee and extends right leg for the throw.

PULLING-DOWN STRAIGHT FOOT—CRAB CLAW THROW

372. Thrower attempts Pulling-down Straight Foot Throw, which is opposed by Receiver who pulls back and squats.

373, 374. Taking advantage of Receiver's backward motion, Thrower executes Crab Claw Throw.

367   368   369

INSIDE SWEEPING FOOT—SHOULDERING THROW

375. Thrower attempts Inside Sweeping Foot Throw, opposed by Receiver.

376, 377. Thrower drops down into position for Shouldering Throw and executes it.

SPRING FOOT—OUTERCUT THROWS

378. Thrower attempts Spring Foot Throw which is opposed by Receiver shifting his weight backward.

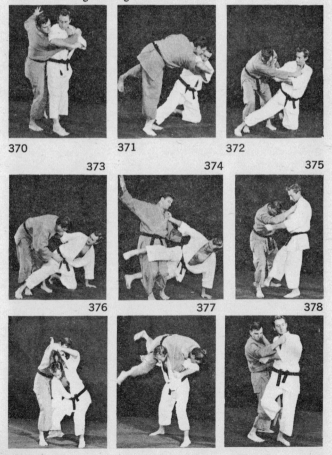

370 371 372

373 374 375

376 377 378

379   380   381

379.   Thrower takes advantage of backward motion to execute
Outercut. Thrower uses same leg for second throw as he used
when attempting first throw, simply sliding the bent leg into position for second throw without placing it on the mat.

MAT TECHNIQUES—CHOKES
REAR SLIDING CHOKE

380.   Thrower is behind Receiver who is sitting or lying on the
mat; with your left arm grip cloth at Receiver's right collar; with
your right hand reach around and grip cloth at his lapel. Apply
choke by pulling down with your right hand as you slide your left
arm around the back.
From lying down position, you can lock your heels into Receiver's
knees, arching him backward as you apply the choke.

REAR LAPEL CHOKE

381.   Thrower is at the rear of Receiver, who is sitting, standing
or lying on mat. Reach around Receiver's neck and grip cloth high
at his lapels with both hands crossed. Choke is applied by pulling
around and back with both arms.

UNDER AND OVER ARM CHOKE

382.   Thrower is behind Receiver (standing, seated or lying on
mat); with your right arm reach around and grip cloth high at his
shoulder; your forearm should be applying pressure at the left side
of his neck, *not* against the windpipe; your left arm can slide under
his left arm, placing your hand at the back of his head; applying
choke by pressing with your left hand.

383.   The variation is to reach over his left arm with your left
arm and placing your fist into the middle of his back; apply choke
by pulling around and back with your right arm.

REAR BARE BODY CHOKE

384.   Thrower is behind Receiver (sitting, standing or lying on
mat). Place your right arm around Receiver's neck with the wind-

pipe into the bend of your elbow (your pressure is *not* against the windpipe); your right hand grips your own left elbow; your left hand is placed at the back of Receiver's head. Pressure is applied by pushing forward with your left hand and tightening the muscles of both arms.

LOOP CHOKE

385.   Thrower faces Receiver, who is standing or kneeling. With both your hands grip cloth at his left lapel. Do not cross your arms. Pull him sharply down and forward.

386.   Maintain your cloth grip with both hands; loop your right arm around his head (your arms are now crossed at the forearms); apply choke by scissoring action with both arms.

MAT TECHNIQUES—ARM LOCKS AND ANKLE LOCK
STRAIGHT ARM LOCK WITH BODY LEVER

Receiver is lying on the mat, face down, his right arm extended. You are seated at his right side, both your hands grip his right wrist,

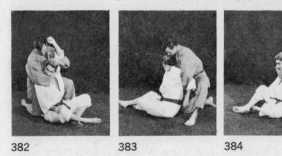

382   383   384

385   386   387

clamping his captured arm under your left arm. Pressure is applied by raising his arm toward his head and leaning in the same direction with your body. 387.

STRAIGHT ARM LOCK WITH LEG LEVER

388.   Receiver is on the mat, face down, his right arm extended; you are on your right side, both hands gripping his wrist; your left leg is crossed over his captured arm at the elbow, your foot braced on the mat, your right leg is wedged into his side. Pressure is applied by raising his captured arm and levering down with your left leg.

STRAIGHT ARM LOCK INTO BODY

389.   Thrower kneels at Receiver's right side; Receiver is on the mat, lying on his right side, his left arm is extended. Lock his left wrist into your neck and shoulder (your left side); place your left forearm over his left elbow; with your right hand grip your own left hand, and pull into your body.

REAR BENT ARM LOCK

390.   Receiver is lying on the mat, face down, his right arm bent behind his back; with your left hand grab his wrist; your right arm reaches under his wrist and grips your own left wrist. Pressure is applied by raising his captured arm toward his head.

ANKLE LOCK

391.   Receiver is on the mat, on his back; you are seated at his feet; his left foot is clamped into your right armpit; your right forearm is under his captured leg at the ankle; your left hand is placed on his shin; your right hand grips your own left wrist. Your left foot is placed at the inside of his right thigh, for brace. Pressure is applied by leaning back slightly and raising your right forearm.

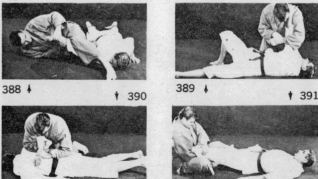

388 ↑   ↑ 390   389 ↑   ↑ 391

BLACK BELT REQUIREMENTS (sho dan)

FORMAL THROWING (naga no kata)

Ceremony and Procedure
Traditional Preliminary Movements

FIRST BLACK BELT THROWS: HAND OR
ARM THROWS (te waza)

1. Pulling-down Throw (uki otoshi)
2. One-Arm Over-Shoulder Throw (seoi-nage)
3. Shouldering Throw (kata guruma)

LOIN OR BODY THROWS (koshi waza)

4. Hip Throw (uki goshi)
5. Sweeping Loin Throw (harai goshi)
6. Levering Arm Hip Throw (tsurikomi goshi)

FOOT OR LEG THROWS (ashi waza)

7. Side Sweeping Foot Throw (okuri ashi harai)
8. Lifting Sweeping Foot Throw (sasae tsurikomi ashi)
9. Upper Innercut Throw (uchi mata)

THROWING WITH THE BACK ON
GROUND (masutemi waza)

10. Circle Throw (tomoe nage)
11. Back Body Sacrifice Throw (ura nage)
12. Inside Lateral Dash Throw (sumi gaeshi)

THROWING WITH THE SIDE ON
GROUND (yoko sutemi waza)

13. Rear Sweeping Foot and Takedown Throw (yoko gake)
14. Side Body Sacrifice Throw (yoko guruma)
15. Ankle Lateral Dash Throw (uki waza)

SYSTEM OF RESUSCITATION (katsu and kappo)

First Aid: Your Responsibility, Moral and Legal
Revival from Unconsciousness
First Aid for Accidental Groin Blow

F

CONTEST (randori)

You must win points in contest against two First-Degree Brown Belt opponents.

Please note: Because the achievement of Black Belt is a very special occasion in the life of a Judo player, it is marked by more formality and ceremony than the lower degrees. The demonstration of forms is more stylized and more ritualistic. The level of contest should be, of course, more skillful and sophisticated.

After the degree of Black Belt has been decided upon, the teacher or judge should make a formal presentation of the belt to the newly promoted player, much in the same manner that a diploma is presented to a newly graduated scholar.

FORMAL THROWING: CEREMONY AND PROCEDURE

The formal demonstration of throws for Black Belt is done in a stylized, prearranged manner, as are all the formal throws for the lower degrees, but the Black Belt formal throws are characterized by more ceremonial procedures. The 15 throws for Black Belt are in 5 sets of 3 throws each. These throws should be repeated on both sides. The types of throws are: arm throws, body throws, foot and leg throws, sacrificing throws with back ending, sacrificing throws with side ending.

Following the formal style of ancient Japanese etiquette, the preliminary movements really have nothing to do with sport. The seated bowing, the repeated bowing to each other and to the symbol of authority is an exaggerated, ceremonial representation of Japanese custom. There is no reason why American and European Judo players cannot modify the preliminary ceremony of the formal throws. Simply bowing to each other should be enough. Custom dictates the older, more complicated preliminary movements, but remember that it is Japanese custom and that each country may substitute preliminary movements which are appropriate to its notions of etiquette, courtesy and sportsmanship. The players could adopt the custom of shaking hands, saluting each other with a bow of the head, or if they prefer something more elaborate, could simply use the gesture of salute as in photos 392, 393.

TRADITIONAL PRELIMINARY MOVEMENTS

394.   Players stand facing, about 12 feet apart (in the photo they are shown closer).

395.   They turn to face the judge, or judges.

396.   In unison, they bow to the judge. They return to facing position.

397.   They kneel on right knee, lowering themselves in a slow, deliberate manner.

392

393

394

395

396

397

398.   They put both knees on the mat.

399.   They sit on their heels, with hands on their thighs.

400.   Placing their hands on the mat, with fingers facing inward, they bow. Women are required to look down as they bow—showing women were thought of as inferior creatures. When two players of unequal rank demonstrate these formal throws, the higher-ranking player looks at the lower-ranking player and the lower-ranking player looks down.

Reversing all the movements, the players then sit up as in photo 399, raise their bodies as in photo 398, rise on one knee as in photo 397, then stand facing as in photo 394. Advancing the left foot first, players take a step at a time (simultaneously) until they are about three feet apart. At this point, they hesitate, then simultaneously take another half step forward (advancing left foot) and are ready to grasp each other in the standard throwing practice manner, photo 401.

PULLING-DOWN THROW

Movements of Thrower and Receiver are coordinated, as in all formal throwing. For Black Belt work, the coordination is expected to be perfect and every move made in unison with precision timing and action. All 15 throws are demonstrated in a continuous, flowing action.

From standard starting position, Thrower (shown right) takes a step forward with his right foot, as Receiver takes a step back with his left foot.

402.   In unison, players reverse the forward motion, Receiver stepping forward with his right foot as Thrower places his left knee down onto the mat (his right foot kept in place).

Using a wheeling motion of his arms, Thrower pulls Receiver around.

403.   Receiver assists in the action by doing #12 fall, ending as shown.

When the throw is completed, both players hesitate for a few seconds in the ending position. Then, while Thrower stays in place, Receiver curls his legs and rolls forward to kneeling position, hesitates and then both players rise into standing position. Repeat throw on other side. In unison, players take sliding, gliding steps in a circular direction until they are both in starting place, about 3 feet apart if they are using New-Style beginning. They should be 12 feet apart if the next throw is being done from the Old-Style starting position.

398

399

400

401

402

403

ONE-ARM OVER-SHOULDER THROW

Here is shown one of the contradictions and discrepancies of formal throwing as practiced in the traditional manner. Although the formal throws are explicitly described as being for sport, exercise and body control, several of the formal techniques begin with an action which is an attack, implying that these techniques are for self-defense. We show here the old-fashioned starting gesture and an adaption, more suitable for sport use, which begins with a stylized gesture indicating an attempt to throw (rather than to attack).

Old-Style: As Thrower stands in place, Receiver begins gesture of overhead fist blow.

404.   As Receiver's arm comes down, Thrower takes a step forward with his right foot and blocks Receiver's forearm with his forearm.

405.   New-Style: Receiver reaches forward as though to grip Thrower's jacket at the left side.

406, 407.   Thrower grips cloth in the usual manner; uses right foot for a step-in pivot and grips cloth at the upper arm, ready to throw.

Thrower executes One-Arm Over-Shoulder Throw.

As Receiver is going down, Thrower steps into "T" position for balance and then steps back into natural stance, which he maintains until Receiver rises to standing position. After throw is completed, players face each other in starting position and repeat throw on the other side. Then both in unison, take sliding, gliding steps in circular direction to return to starting position, within arm's reach, ready for next throw.

SHOULDERING THROW

408.   Players grip cloth in unison.

409.   As Thrower steps forward with his right foot into position to apply Shouldering Throw, Receiver takes a short step back with his left foot to allow Thrower to take hold.

410.   Throw is executed and Receiver assists the action and falls in usual manner. Thrower stands in place while Receiver rises first to kneeling and then to standing position. Repeat throw on other side. They take gliding steps in unison in circular direction to return to starting position within arm's reach if using New-Style beginning. They should be about 12 feet part, if using Old-Style beginning.

HIP THROW

411.   New-Style: As Receiver takes a short step with his right foot and reaches out with his right hand, Thrower starts to pivot with his right foot as he grips cloth with his right hand.

412.   Old-Style: Players take steps in unison, advancing left foot first. On the second step, Receiver makes a gesture of overhead fist blow, and Thrower sidesteps the blow and grips cloth.

404

405

406

407

408

409

410

411

412

413.   Thrower pivots clockwise into position for Hip Throw on the left side, as shown.

Thrower executes the throw, taking "T" position for balance, then returns to natural stance which he maintains while Receiver rises to standing position. Repeat throw on the other side. Then both in unison, take sliding, gliding steps in circular direction to return to starting position, within arm's reach, ready for next throw.

SWEEPING LOIN THROW

414.   From a standstill, players grip cloth in unison.

415.   Thrower pivots into position, counterclockwise.

416.   Thrower executes Sweeping Loin Throw, which Receiver assists by springing up slightly as throw is applied.

Repeat throw on other side. At completion of throw, as before, players return to starting position, within arm's reach, ready for the next throw.

LEVERING ARM HIP THROW

From standstill, players grip in unison.

417.   Thrower pivots into position for a Neck Throw, as Receiver crouches and bends back slightly.

418.   Thrower then shifts to a very low Hip Throw position and grips cloth at the back of Receiver's collar, keeping right arm stiff and straight.

419.   Thrower applies Hip Throw with the aid of a levering arm action against Receiver's neck as throw is executed; springing up as he applies the throw gives Thrower added thrust motion.

Repeat throw on other side. At the completion of the throw, both players return, as before, to starting position within arm's reach, ready for the next throw.

SIDE SWEEPING FOOT THROW

420.   After hesitating in the starting position, players take sliding steps (in unison) in a circular direction once.

421, 422.   As Receiver takes another sliding step, Thrower places his left foot in position for Side Sweeping Foot Throw and executes the throw as Receiver's feet come together at the end of step. Both feet are swept in this throw and Receiver allows the momentum of his sliding steps to assist the action.

Repeat throw on other side. At the completion of the throw, both players return to starting position, within arm's reach.

413

414

415

416

417

418

419

420

421

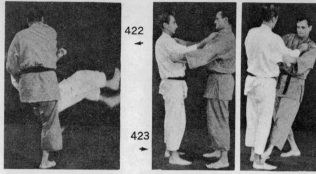

LIFTING SWEEPING FOOT THROW

423.   Players grip cloth in unison.

424.   After a slight hesitation, Thrower pulls Receiver forward causing him to take a short step forward with his right foot, onto which Thrower places his left foot (high on the instep, near the ankle).

425.   With the assistance of a springing action from the Receiver, Thrower executes throw.

Repeat throw on other side. After the completion of the throw, players face each other in starting position and repeat throw on the other side. Glide-step, as before, into starting position, within arm's reach, ready for next throw.

UPPER INNERCUT THROW

426, 427, 428.   Taking sliding steps in unison, players make a 180° change in the starting position so that players' starting position is exactly reversed. This is done in two large steps.

429, 430.   As Receiver takes a third circular step, Thrower applies Upper Innercut Throw.

Repeat throw on other side. After the completion of the throw, players return to starting position, within arm's reach, ready for the next throw.

CIRCLE THROW

431.   As Thrower takes a step forward on his right foot, Receiver takes a step backward with his left foot.

432.   As Thrower places his right foot at Receiver's belt and pulls back, Receiver rocks his body forward.

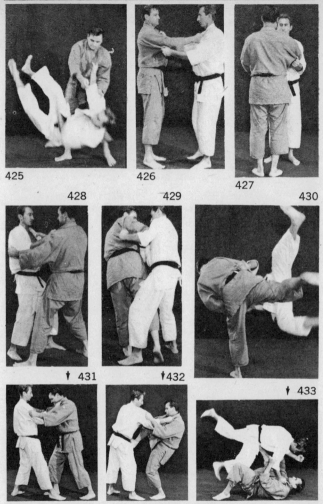

425   426   427

428   429   430

↓ 431   ↑432   ↑ 433

433. As Thrower applies the Circle Throw, Receiver continues his forward movement to assist the action of the throw.

At the completion of the throw, both players return to starting position and repeat the throw on the other side. Return to starting position within arm's reach (if using New-Style form) or about 12 feet apart (if using Old-Style form), ready for the next throw.

BACK BODY SACRIFICE THROW

434. Old-Style: Facing (at about 12-foot distance), Thrower stays in place while Receiver begins gesture of downward fist blow.

New-Style: Players stand facing, within arm's reach. Receiver makes gesture of reaching to grip as if to throw.

435. As Receiver takes a deep step forward and brings his fist down, Thrower takes a deep step forward to Receiver's right side and places his hands at Receiver's back and stomach.

436. This photo is an insert to show you the position of the hands (the body positions are not correct).

437. Locking Receiver's body in tightly, Thrower twists his own body counterclockwise and leans back.

438. The throw is completed by Thrower falling directly upon his back as he twists Receiver off to the left, and down.

After throw is completed, players rise to face each other and repeat the throw on the other side. Rise and return to starting position, within arm's reach, ready for the next throw.

INSIDE LATERAL DASH THROW

Players begin in standard position, within arm's reach.

439. Old-Style: In unison, players grip cloth and lock their heads at each other's right shoulder, as shown; both taking a step forward with the right foot.

New-Style: Because the Old-Style beginning stance has no relation to the usual actions of sport Judo, but rather simulates an old-fashioned wrestling-type attack, the variation which can be used instead eliminates the head-on-neck action; both players simply take a step forward with the right foot and grip cloth in customary fashion.

440. Thrower lowers himself to the mat, as he slides his left leg so that it blocks Receiver's right ankle; Thrower's right instep lifts Receiver's left leg at the inside of the knee; Thrower's arms continuously pull and thrust Receiver over Thrower's head.

After throw is completed, players rise to face each other in starting position and repeat throw on the other side. Then they rise to return to starting position, within arm's reach, ready for the next throw.

REAR SWEEPING FOOT AND TAKEDOWN THROW

441. From standard starting position, Thrower twists Receiver (counterclockwise) so that Receiver's side is toward Thrower; Thrower takes a step with his right foot as he twists.

434   435   436

437   438   439

440

441

442, 443. Thrower applies Rear Sweeping Foot Throw, with this variation—the lifting foot is carried forward very high and the Thrower falls backward with the Receiver, releasing his grip just in time to slap the mat.

Both players rise to starting position and repeat the throw on the other side. Then, both players rise and return to starting position within arm's reach (New-Style) or 12 feet apart (Old-Style), ready for the next throw.

SIDE BODY SACRIFICE THROW

444. Old-Style: Receiver takes a very deep step in and threatens Thrower with overhand fist blow.

New-Style: Receiver reaches forward as though to grip cloth for throw.

445. Thrower sidesteps and grips Receiver's body at back and abdomen.

446, 447. Thrower slides right foot between Receiver's feet, twisting his body and falling toward his left side. Receiver is taken over by Thrower's arms pulling him and by momentum of Thrower's body falling down.

Thrower releases his grip only when Receiver begins his rolling fall.

Both players rise to starting position and repeat throw on the other side. Then both players rise to face each other within arm's reach, ready for the final throw of the group.

ANKLE LATERAL DASH THROW

448. Old-Style: Players simulate wrestling stance.

New-Style: Players grip cloth in unison.

449, 450. Thrower executes Lateral Dash Throw with this variation from the standard throw—instead of placing his foot upon Receiver's instep, he blocks Receiver's ankle with his ankle.

442

443

When throw is completed, both players rise to repeat the throw on the other side. Then, both players rise to starting position.

451. Taking steps backward in unison, players take position about 12 feet apart (in the photo they are shown closer). The beginning ceremony is repeated, in reverse order.

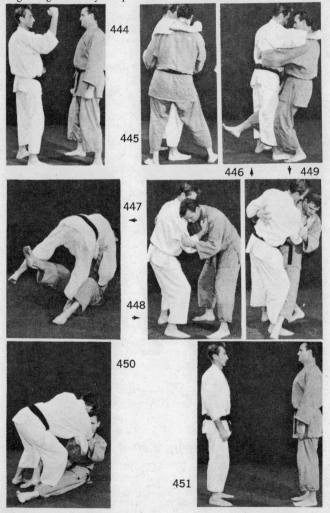

FIRST AID: RESPONSIBILITY, MORAL AND LEGAL

Where proper safety precautions are taken, accidents in Judo practice are neither serious nor frequent. In tournament, accidents are
more likely to occur because in the intense atmosphere of competition and excitement, players become more reckless. This is
true of most body-contact sports. A doctor should be present at
any open contest. If you engage in group practice, even on a
friendly, club basis, you should have the telephone number of a
doctor or hospital on hand so that you do not lose valuable time
in the event of any emergency.

Although it is much preferred to have professional medical help
available, advanced Judo players should be familiar with routine
techniques of first aid which apply to possible practice accidents:
sprains, dislocations, breaks and unconsciousness. I advise people
who are engaged in regular Judo practice to take a course in first
aid, which most communities offer free of charge.

There are two important factors to be considered when faced with
an emergency situation—your moral obligation and your legal
position. Sometimes these two factors are in opposition and you
will have to make a choice. If you give some thought to this problem beforehand, you can avoid acting in panic and assure the
injured person the best chance of needed care.

If you attempt first aid on an injured person and that person can
be proved to have suffered additional injury from your well-meant
but inadequate attentions, you are in a legal position of being responsible for his worsened condition. Therefore, it is greatly to be
desired that professional medical care be made available *if at all
possible*. If, for some reason beyond your control, you are unable
to get in touch with a doctor, or with anyone who can get a doctor
(police, fire department, emergency hospital), and you have *only*
the choice of trying to help the injured person or allowing him to
remain altogether neglected, then your clear moral duty is to apply
whatever knowledge you have in an effort to assist him. You
should be warned, again, that trying to assist an injured person
without having first-aid training is more likely to result in aggra-
vating the injury than in giving aid.

The following techniques of resuscitation and first aid are not
ordinarily taught in conventional American first-aid classes. They
are taught and successfully used by advanced Judo players. Their
use is subject to the same conditions as described above.

REVIVAL FROM UNCONSCIOUSNESS

Even when unconciousness is the result of a legal choke (against
the carotid artery), there is danger of serious injury if the player
is not revived within a short time. Depending upon the individual,
brain damage could occur within 30 minutes.

452. For a person in a groggy state, not altogether unconscious, but not functioning normally, place him in a seated position and strike sharply in a downward direction hitting between the shoulder blades. Use the heel of your palm for striking and strike so that the pressure of the blow goes in the direction of his abdomen. Repeat once or twice. Loosen his belt and let him lie down and revive.

In addition, if unconsciousness is the result of a choke, massage the sides of his neck in an upward direction.

Usually, an unconscious person is limp and relaxed. Occasionally, however, he may stiffen and become very rigid. In this event, be very carefully how you move him; do not try to *force* arms or legs from the rigid position, but very gently move them. Forcing against a rigid arm or leg could result in injury.

453. Place the unconscious person on his back, moving him gently. Place the heels of your palms just below his rib cage. With a sharp movement, press and release. The direction of the pressure is toward his feet, not toward the mat. Repeat once or twice.

454. If he does not revive in a moment or two from the above, kneel at his legs and place yours in a "Y" position just above the pelvic area. With a sharp movement, press upward and release. The direction of the pressure is toward his shoulders. Repeat once or twice.

In addition, if unconsciousness is the result of a choke, massage the sides of his neck in an upward direction.

455. Place unconscious person in a seated position, moving him

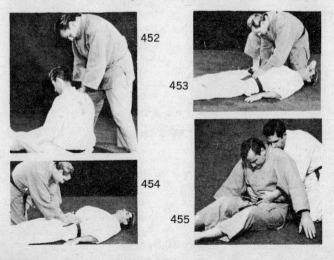

452

453

454

455

very gently. Kneel at his back with your knee in the center of his back between the shoulder blades. Put your arms under his arms and interlace your fingers, placing your hands just above the pelvic area. With a sharp movement, pull up with your hands and release. The upward motion is in the direction of your knee. Repeat once or twice.

In addition, if unconsciousness is the result of choking, massage the sides of his neck in an upward direction.

FIRST AID FOR ACCIDENTAL GROIN BLOW

Following are three first-aid techniques to be used in the event of accidental blow to the testicles.

LIGHT BLOW

This technique is used when only a light blow has hit the testicles.

456.   Place yourself in a natural stance and leap up with both feet.

457.   With your legs slightly bent, but rigid and spread apart, land on your heels so that your body is jarred. Repeat once or twice. Massage your lower abdomen in a downward direction.

REVIVAL FROM UNCONSCIOUSNESS (1)

A heavy blow to the testicles will sometimes force them up into the body as well as cause unconsciousness. The first technique is meant to effect release of the testicles. After that has been accomplished, apply any of the other techniques for revival *except those* which utilize the upward striking action.

458.   Place the person on his back, handling him very gently. Kneel at his leg and grip his big toe and raise his leg up (as shown) and slightly outward.

459.   With the heel of your fist, strike sharply at the heel of his held foot. The direction of your blow is from his heel to his hip socket. Repeat once or twice. Repeat on the other leg, if necessary.

Massage his lower abdomen in a downward direction.

REVIVAL FROM UNCONSCIOUSNESS (2)

This technique is meant to release the testicles. If the person has not regained consciousness after this is done, apply any of the other revival techniques *except* those which strike in an upward direction.

460.   Unconscious person is in a seated position, legs slightly spread. From a crouching position behind him, lock your forearms under his arms.

461.   Raise him off the mat, as shown.

462.   Allow him to drop; standing close behind him so that he does not fall backward. If necessary, repeat once or twice.

Massage his lower abdomen in a downward direction.

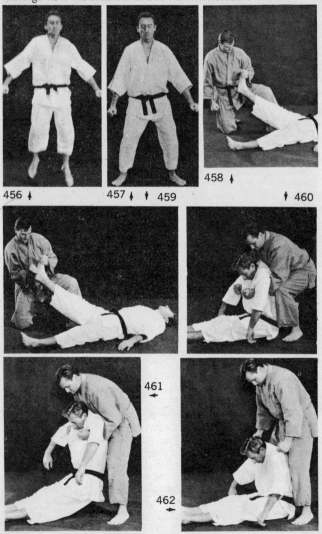

456 ↟   457 ↟ ↡ 459   ↡ 460

458 ↟

461
←

462
→

PART THREE

FORMAL THROWS FOR BELT DEGREES—OLD STYLE

INTRODUCTION TO FORM DEGREES

While it is not generally known today, Dr. Kano, the founder of Judo, placed as much importance upon the development of skill in the forms of Judo as he did upon contest skill. Contest is more exciting and spectacular; competition, in all its forms, is so much encouraged in our society that it is natural that the competitive aspect of Judo has been encouraged over the relatively passive formal work. As a result, only the most aggressive and combative individuals have been induced to take up the sport of Judo. This is too bad, because there are many individuals who could and should be encouraged to practice Judo without being required to compete. There are those whose natural style it is to prefer accomplishment of a personal kind, who do not get a thrill out of body-contact contest, but who get tremendous satisfaction from body-discipline skills; there are women, to whom the idea of contest is either silly or repugnant; there are people whose physical makeup prevents them from ever becoming superior in active contest; there are the older people; and, finally, there are those people to whom the once-a-week practice of Judo is simply a pleasant part of an otherwise very full life. These people have not the time, interest, temperament or physical ability to become Judo champions, or even very competent Judo contestants.

The custom of requiring contest of all students has been a major factor in driving new people away from Judo. The alternative to contest is form work for those people who wish to increase their Judo knowledge, take pleasure in learning Judo, benefit from the wholesome exercise of Judo and achieve Judo belt degrees. The forms are good exercise and good fun. They can be done by small and large people, by young and old, by men and women.

The forms are a prearranged, stylized manner of performing the techniques of Judo. In the Old-Style forms, there is a mixture of sport and self-defense techniques which formerly had validity, but since most of the techniques of self-defense relate to an outmoded style of life, we can look upon all of them as having the same purpose—the development of coordination, dexterity, balance, grace and muscle tone. The timing and precision which are required for performing the bits of ceremony are as useful as learning to dance . . . they lead to better control of our body movements, giving a more poised body attitude.

The student who earns his or her degree in forms of Judo is not to be looked down upon as having an "inferior" degree. It is a different, but not an inferior kind of achievement, which is being recognized and rewarded by promotion in the belting ranks. The form degree student has had to work just as hard as the contest degree student and should be just as proud of his accomplishment.

REQUIREMENTS FOR DEGREES

Green Belt: Same requirement as in competition degrees.

Third Brown Belt: Formal throws (nage-no-kata). Same as Black Belt requirements of competition degrees.

Second Brown Belt: Mat-work forms (katame-no-kata)—women substitute the New-Style forms.

First Brown Belt: Counterthrow forms (gonosen-no-kata).

First Black Belt: Old-Style self-defense forms (kime-no-kata).

MOVEMENTS FOR CEREMONIAL PROCEDURES

The movements for forms are quite different from the movements in free-style practice and for contest. In contest, speed and strategy are necessary as well as technical knowledge; in the forms, technique is demonstrated without opposition from the partner and there is a slower, more deliberate mode of work. Everything is prearranged, stylized, choreographed one might say. All the body actions are timed for smooth, flowing, eloquent kinesis. Where it is indicated that both players move in unison, there should be perfect synchronization of the actions.

The steps which the players take when coming onto the mat, when moving into position for demonstration for the technique, when returning after completion of one technique to begin the next technique—these are all formal, slow—almost theatrical. No casual, ambling movements are permitted; even the little hesitations between parts of the forms, at the end of forms, etc., are made in a dramatic style.

Some schools favor a gliding, sliding type of step for all the walking action required in forms; other schools prefer a slow-motion walk. Both are correct; it is a matter of preference.

The ceremony for the New-Style forms is more simple than for the Old-Style forms. Enough ceremony is retained to emphasize the fact that *perfection of technique* is the essence of the forms.

SECOND-DEGREE BROWN BELT REQUIREMENTS (nikyu): FORM DEGREE

MAT-WORK FORMS (katame-no-kata):

First Set—Holds (osea waza)

1. Side Shoulder Hold (kesa-gatame)
2. Side Shoulder Hold with Arm Lock (kata-gatame)
3. Smother Hold (kami-shiho-gatame)
4. Cross Body Hold with Head and Leg Lock (yoko-shiho-gatame)
5. Top Body Hold with Arm Lock (kami-shiho-gatami)

Second Set—Chokes (shime waza)

1. Cross Arm Choke (kata-juji-jime)
2. Rear One-Arm Choke (hadaka-jime)
3. Rear Lapel Choke (okuri-eri-jime)
4. Choke with Half Nelson (kata ha jime)
5. Cross Arm Choke with Foot Leverage (gyaku-yoko-juji-jime)

Third Set—Locks (kensetsu waza)

1. Bent Arm Lock (ude-garami)
2. Straight Arm Lock with Hip Pressure (ude-hishigi-juji gatame)
3. Straight Arm Lock with Shoulder Pressure
   (ude-hishigi-ude-gatame)
4. Straight Arm Lock with Leg Pressure (ude-hishigi-hiza gatame)
5. Sitting-down Two-Arm Lock (ashi-garami)

Please note: Mat-work forms are not appropriate for women students and are not required for women who are working for promotion to Second Degree Brown Belt. Instead, substitute the New-Style self-defense form.

SIDE SHOULDER HOLD

Both men stand facing, about 12 feet apart. In unison, both men kneel; bow. Both men rise to one knee, right foot on mat; Receiver pivots on left knee and lies down on the mat with his head toward you; as Receiver lies down, you rise, walk over to him and kneel on your left knee, as shown in photo 463. Receiver is passive throughout the form, acting merely as a demonstration body. Without rising, slide toward Receiver so that you are close to his side.

464.   With your right hand place Receiver's right arm under your left arm.

465.   Reach around his neck with your right hand and assume position of Side Shoulder Hold. Hesitate for a moment, to demonstrate proper technique.

Return to kneeling position at Receiver's side.

SIDE SHOULDER HOLD WITH ARM LOCK

466. From starting kneeling position, begin to apply the regular Side Shoulder Hold.

467. Push Receiver's right arm across his face.

468. Place Receiver's right arm over your right shoulder, locking it there between your head and shoulder; hesitate.

Return to starting position.

463

464

465

466

467

468

SMOTHER HOLD (TOP BODY HOLD)

469.   From starting kneeling position, you rise, walk around to Receiver's head, kneel.

470, 471.   Slide both your hands under Receiver's shoulders, then along his body to grip his belt; lock your elbows firmly into his sides; assume position of Smother Hold (See p. 117 for details of instruction); hesitate, to show proper technique.

Rise and return to kneeling position at Receiver's side.

CROSS BODY HOLD WITH HEAD AND LEG LOCK

472.   From starting position you begin to apply regular Cross Body Hold (see p. 115 for instructions), reaching under Receiver's bent left leg.

473.   With your right hand, grip Receiver's belt at the side; with your right hand reach around his head and grip his collar. Hesitate, to show proper technique.

Rise and return to starting kneeling position .

TOP BODY HOLD WITH ARM LOCK

From starting kneeling position at Receiver's side, you rise and walk around to his head, kneel.

474, 475.   With your left hand, raise Receiver's right arm and lock in under your right armpit with your elbow, gripping cloth with your right hand; apply Top Body Hold; hold for a moment to show proper technique; rise and return to starting kneeling position at Receiver's side. After a moment's hesitation, you slide away from Receiver (about one foot).

Both rise and walk to face each other about 12 feet apart; both kneel onto left knee. At this point, both men may retie belt, if necessary, straighten jackets and are then ready to continue to second set of mat-work forms.

CROSS ARM CHOKE

To begin second set of mat-work forms, both rise and return to position with Receiver lying on the mat and you kneeling at his side.

476.   With your left hand grip Receiver's left collar (thumb outside of jacket).

477.   As you straddle Receiver, grip his right collar with your right hand.

478.   Apply Cross Arm Choke (simulated) as you place your head on the mat next to Receiver's head. Hold position for a moment to demonstrate proper technique; return to starting kneeling position at side.

469

470

471

472

473

474

475

476

477

478

REAR ONE-ARM CHOKE

Note that this is a windpipe choke, which is dangerous to apply with force. You must *gently simulate* the action in this form, or you will hurt your partner.

479.   From starting kneeling position at Receiver's side, you walk around and kneel at his head (about two feet behind him) as he rises to sitting position.

480.   On your knees, you slide up directly to Receiver.

481, 482.   With your right forearm placed around his neck, grip your right wrist with your left hand; place your head onto his left shoulder; *simulate* choking action; maintain position for a moment to demonstrate proper technique.

Release choke, return to kneeling position behind Receiver (as in photo 480).

REAR LAPEL CHOKE

483.   With your left hand reach under Receiver's left arm and grip cloth at his right lapel.

484, 485.   With your right hand reach over his shoulder and grip cloth at his left shoulder; simulate choking action by levering back with both hands; maintain position for a moment to demonstrate proper technique.

Release choke, stay in kneeling position behind Receiver.

CHOKE WITH HALF NELSON

486.   Slide your left hand under Receiver's left arm.

487.   Place your left hand behind Receiver's head; with your right hand reach around Receiver's neck and grip cloth at his left collar; pressure is applied (simulated) by straightening out both arms. Hold simulated choking position for a moment to demonstrate correct technique.

As Receiver lies down, you rise, walk around to Receiver's side; kneel.

CROSS ARM CHOKE WITH FOOT LEVERAGE

488.   With your left hand grip cloth at Receiver's left collar.

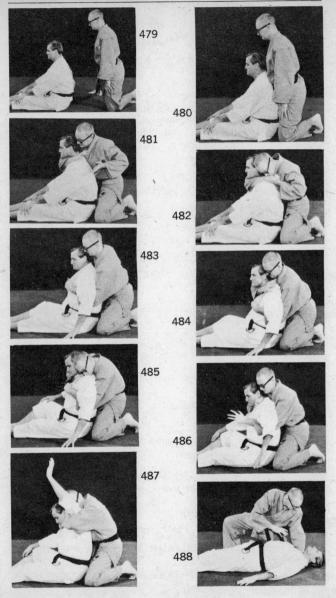

479
480
481
482
483
484
485
486
487
488

489.   Straddle Receiver as you grip cloth at his right collar with your right hand.

490.   Applying choking pressure (simulated) as you roll over Receiver's left side.

491.   Receiver has followed rolling motion with his body; with Receiver in position shown, simulate choking pressure, adding leverage of foot pressure, placing both your feet at his belt; maintain position to show correct technique; return to kneeling at side starting position; hesitate; return to kneeling facing position to start next set of forms.

BENT ARM LOCK

492.   Return to starting kneeling position at Receiver's side. Receiver raises his left hand; with your left hand, block the raised arm.

493.   Grip Receiver's raised arm at the wrist with your left hand and bend it toward his shoulder; start to reach under the captured arm with your right hand.

494.   Grip your own left wrist with your right hand as you place yourself across Receiver's body; apply lock by pulling both arms toward yourself; hold position for a moment to show correct form; return to starting position.

STRAIGHT ARM LOCK WITH HIP PRESSURE

495.   Receiver raises his right arm; start to grip raised wrist with both your hands.

496.   As you grip his wrist, sit down and place your left leg across Receiver's neck.

497.   Lie back onto the mat, wedge your right foot into Receiver's side; bring his captured arm across your thigh; apply pressure (simulated) by raising up with your hips; maintain hold to show correct technique; return to starting position.

STRAIGHT ARM LOCK WITH SHOULDER PRESSURE

498.   Receiver raises his left arm; start to grip his raised arm at the elbow with both your hands.

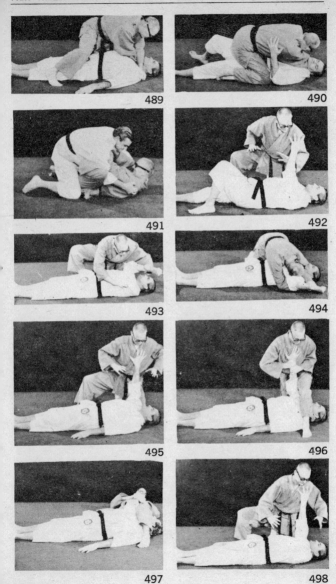

499. Keeping his captured arm straight, pull it into your chest and lock it into your body as you lever forward with your shoulder; hold position for a moment to show correct technique; return to starting kneeling position.

STRAIGHT ARM LOCK WITH LEG PRESSURE

500. From kneeling position at side of Receiver, both rise in unison to face within arm's reach; kneel; grip cloth in standard throwing fashion.

501. Simulate a heel-of-palm blow into Receiver's face; Receiver releases right hand cloth grip.

502. Capture Receiver's right hand under your left arm and lock it into your body as you place your right foot at his left knee.

503. Push his knee as you roll to your right side; cross your left leg over his captured arm; simulate action by pushing with your right foot as you lever downward with your left leg; hold position to show correct technique; return to kneeling position, facing, hesitate.

SITTING-DOWN TWO-ARM LOCK

504. From kneeling facing position, rise in unison and grip each other in standard throwing fashion.

505. Sit down between Receiver's feet; placing your right foot at his belt.

506. Both your hands grip cloth at his elbows; press in with your arms to lock his arms; place your left foot at his right side (note that it is curled around the outside of his leg).

507. 508. As you topple Receiver forward with your legs (off toward your right side) maintain your hold on his arms and twist them. Pressure is applied by pressing into his body with your left leg, locking his leg; forcing his head and shoulder into the mat; both his arms remain locked and straight. Hold position for a moment to show correct technique. Rise in unison to kneeling position about 12 feet apart; both rise and reverse the starting ceremonial procedures, ending with a bow to the judge (or teacher).

FIRST-DEGREE BROWN BELT REQUIREMENTS
(ikkyu): FORM DEGREE

COUNTERTHROW FORMS (gonosen-no-kata)

1. Kickback Throw (osoto-gari) with Counter of Kickback Throw
2. Kneecap Throw with Counter of Kneecap Throw (hiza-guruma)
3. Innercut Throw with Counter of Back Sweeping Foot Throw (o-uchi-gari and ko-soto-gari)

499

500

501

502

503

504

505

506

507

508

4. Front Sweeping Foot Throw with Counter of Front Sweeping Foot Throw (de-ashi-barai)

5. Outercut Throw with Counter of Straight Foot Throw (ko-soto-gake and tai-otoshi)

6. Inside Sweeping Foot Throw with Counter of Lifting Sweeping Foot Throw (ko-uchi-gari and harai-tsurikomi-ashi)

7. Neck Throw with Counter of Rear Hip Throw (koshi-guruma and ushiro-goshi)

8. Hip Throw with Counter of Left Side Hip Throw (tsurikomi-goshi and uki-goshi)

9. Spring Foot Throw with Counter of Lifting Sweeping Foot Throw (hane-goshi and harai-tsurikomi-ashi)

10. Sweeping Loin Throw with Counter of Rear Hip Throw (harai-goshi and ushiro-goshi)

11. Upper Innercut with Counter of Rear Hip Throw (uchi-mata and ushiro-goshi)

12. Over-Shoulder Throw with Counter of Inside Lateral Dash (seoi-nage and sumi-gaeshi)

KICKBACK THROW

This set of forms is begun in the same fashion as the throwing forms. Thrower and Receiver begin the actual forms facing, in standard throwing position. Receiver simulates the first throw (without actually attempting to execute the throw) and Thrower in each instance, counters with a throw to completion.

509.   Receiver (left) simulates Kickback Throw.

510.   Thrower counters with Kickback Throw. When Receiver is on the mat, they hesitate for a moment; return to starting position.

KNEECAP THROW

511. Receiver simulates Kneecap Throw.

512.   Thrower counters with Kneecap Throw. When Receiver is on the mat, they hesitate, return to starting position.

INNERCUT THROW

513.   Receiver simulates Innercut Throw.

514.   Thrower counters with Back Sweeping Foot Throw. When Receiver is on the mat, they hesitate; return to starting position.

FRONT SWEEPING FOOT THROW

515.   Receiver simulates Front Sweeping Foot Throw.

516.   Thrower counters with the same throw. When Receiver is on the mat, both hesitate; return to starting position.

OUTERCUT THROW

517.   Receiver simulates Outercut Throw.

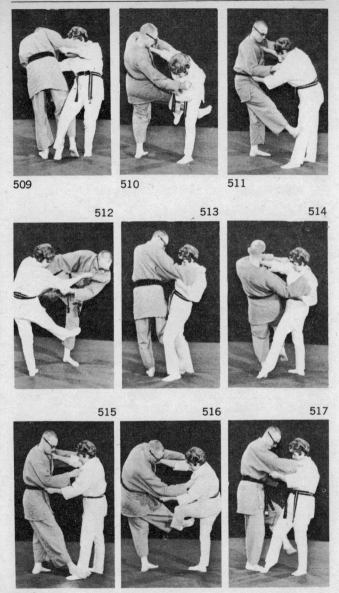

509   510   511

512   513   514

515   516   517

G

518. Thrower executes counter of Straight Foot Throw. After hesitation, both return to starting position.

INSIDE SWEEPING FOOT THROW

519. Receiver simulates Inside Sweeping Foot Throw.

520. Thrower counters with Lifting Sweeping Foot Throw.

NECK THROW

521. Receiver simulates Neck Throw.

522. Thrower counters with Rear Hip Throw.

HIP THROW

523. Receiver simulates Hip Throw.

524. Thrower executes counter of Left Side Hip Throw.

SPRING FOOT THROW

525. Receiver simulates Spring Foot Throw.

526. Thrower counters with Lifting Sweeping Foot Throw.

SWEEPING LOIN THROW

527. Receiver simulates Sweeping Loin Throw.

528. Thrower counters with Rear Hip Throw.

UPPER INNERCUT

529. Receiver simulates Upper Innercut Throw.

518   519   520

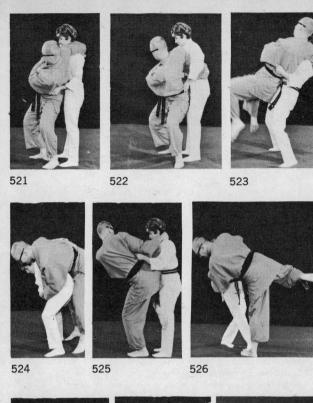

521 522 523

524 525 526

527 528 529

530   531   532

530. Thrower counters with Rear Hip Throw.

OVER-SHOULDER THROW

531. Receiver attempts an Over-Shoulder Throw. Thrower goes over Receiver's hip and simulates an incomplete throw.

532. Thrower then counters with Inside Lateral Dash Throw. After usual moment of hesitation to demonstrate good ending technique, both return to starting position; they reverse the opening ceremonial bowing procedure before leaving the mat.

FIRST-DEGREE BLACK BELT REQUIREMENTS (sho dan): FORM DEGREE

OLD-STYLE SELF-DEFENSE FORMS (kime-no-kata)
Ceremonial Procedure

FIRST SET—SEATED ATTACKS (idori)
1. Two-Hand Grip (ryote-dori)
2. Midsection Blow (tsuk-kake)
3. Open Hand Face Blow (suri-age)
4. Temple Blow (yoko-uchi)
5. Back Grab (ushiro-dori)
6. Dagger Thrust (tsuki-komi)
7. Overhead Dagger Thrust (kiri-komi)
8. Dagger Side Thrust (yoko-tsuki)

SECOND SET—STANDING ATTACKS (tachiai)
1. Two-Hand Grip (ryote-dori)
2. Shoulder Grab (sode-tori)
3. Straight Punch (tsuki-kake)
4. Uppercut (tsuki-agi)
5. Heel-of-Palm Blow (suri-age)
6. Hammer Blow (yoko-uchi)
7. Groin Kick (ke-age)
8. Standing Body Grab (ushiro-dori)
9. Standing Dagger (Thrust (tsuki-komi)

10. Overhead Dagger Thrust (kiri-komi)
11. Sword Drawing (nuki-kake)
12. Standing Overhead Sword (kiri-oroshi)

SYSTEM OF RESUSCITATION (katsu and kappo)

See pp.176-179.

Please note: Because the achievement of Black Belt is a very special occasion in the life of a Judo player, it is marked by more formality and ceremony than the lower degrees. The demonstration of forms is more stylized and more ritualistic.

After the degree of Black Belt has been decided upon, the teacher or judge should make a formal presentation of the belt to the newly promoted player, much in the same manner that a diploma is presented to a newly graduated scholar.

OLD-STYLE SELF-DEFENSE FORMS
CEREMONIAL PROCEDURE

All form movements in the ceremonial procedure are slow and deliberate; partners walk in unison when they are required to move from one spot to another at the same time; they hold their bodies very erect.

Both partners walk onto the mat and stand facing each other about 12 feet apart. Attacker holds the sword and dagger which he will use later in the forms (photo 533). They turn in unison to face the judge (or teacher) and bow to him in unison; they turn and bow to each other. Attacker turns about and walks to the edge of the mat behind him; he kneels in a formal fashion and places the dagger and knife at the edge of the mat (photo 534). Attacker rises, turns, walks to face Defender (about 12 feet away); taking steps in unison, they walk to within 3 feet of each other; in unison they kneel in formal fashion; they slide on their knees to get within arm's reach (photo 535). From this position, they are ready to begin the series of Old-Style self-defense forms which follow.

533

534

535

TWO-HAND GRIP (ryote-dori)

536.   Partners are in seated (kneeling) position. Attacker (left) grips both wrists of Defender.

537.   Defender rises onto knees and kicks with right foot into Attacker's solar plexus as she brings her arms up and outward. She then brings her arms inward, frees her left hand and grips Attacker's left wrist with her left hand.

538.   Defender pivots on her right knee, places her left foot on the mat, draws Attacker's captured arm under her right arm, clamping it close to her body.

Pressure is applied by levering up against the wrist and down onto the elbow. Attacker taps for release when arm lock is applied. Both return to starting, seated position.

MIDSECTION BLOW (tsuk-kake)

539.   Attacker threatens punch into Defender's midsection.

540.   Defender rises onto left knee, turns clockwise a quarter turn, places right foot on mat; as turn is made, Defender strikes with right hand into Attacker's face and grips his right wrist with left hand, pulling Attacker forward, off-balance.

541.   Defender pivots on left knee, making another quarter turn clockwise. As she turns, she grips his captured wrist with her right hand, releasing her grip with the left hand and drawing his arm across her body. With her left hand, Defender reaches around Attacker's throat and grips cloth at his right lapel.

Pressure is applied by levering back with her right hand and pulling cloth against his throat with her left hand. Attacker taps for release when pressure is applied. Both return to seated starting position.

OPEN HAND FACE BLOW (suri-age)

Attacker threatens open-hand face blow.

542.   As Attacker's arm comes forward, Defender rises onto knees and parries the intended blow upward with right hand and with her left hand grips cloth at his right armpit.

543, 544.   Defender kicks into the solar plexus with right foot. Then, she grips his right wrist with her right hand and pivots on her left knee to make a 90° turn, pulling Attacker forward and

544   **545**

down on his face as she turns. His captured arm is kept fully extended, palm up.

545.   Defender slides left knee up onto captured elbow and presses down with the knee, pulling up with the right hand. Attacker taps for release when pressure is applied. Both return to seated starting position.

TEMPLE BLOW (yoko-uchi)

546.   From kneeling position, Attacker begins fist blow to temple.

547.   Defender rises to left knee, steps in with right foot under the blow; grips Attacker around the body.

548.   Using shoulder and body movement Defender throws Attacker to the mat.

549.   Defender simulates elbow blow into midsection. Both return to starting kneeling position.

BACK GRAB (ushiro-dori)

550.   From facing kneeling position, Attacker rises, steps around behind Defender, kneels, as shown.

551.   Attacker grabs around the body.

552.   With both hands, Defender grips cloth at Attacker's right shoulder (as for One-Arm Over-Shoulder Throw).

553.   Defender pulls Attacker down and around onto the mat.

554.   Defender rolls counterclockwise into seated position on Attacker's chest; simulating punch with right fist into the midsection.

Both rise to return to seated kneeling position.

546

547

548

549

550   551   552

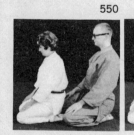

553   554

DAGGER THRUST (tsuki-komi)

From seated starting position, Attacker rises, takes formalized steps to edge of mat; he takes small dagger and returns to starting kneeling position, placing dagger (in scabbard) inside his jacket.

555.   Attacker simulates straight out thrust with dagger.

556.   Defender rises to left knee, pivots clockwise, parrying and grabbing his arm, pulling it forward and past her body; then Defender punches into Attacker's face.

557.   Defender continues pull forward at Attacker's arm, grabs his wrist with her right hand and levers the captured arm over her bent leg; as this is done, she reaches around his neck with her left hand, gripping cloth at his right lapel; choking action is simulated by pulling back with both arms.

Both rise and return to kneeling position; Attacker places dagger in scabbard.

OVERHEAD DAGGER THRUST (kiri-komi)

558.   Attacker simulates beginning overhead dagger thrust.

559.   Defender rises to both knees, gripping hitting arm at the wrist with both hands.

560.   Defender pivots on left knee, placing right foot on mat; as she pivots she pulls his captured arm up under her left arm and locks it into her body.

After hesitating, both rise and return to starting kneeling position.

DAGGER SIDE THRUST (yoko-tsuki)

561.   From seated kneeling position, facing, Attacker rises, steps around to kneel at right side of Defender.

562.   Attacker simulates sideward dagger thrust.

563.   Defender rises to left knee, pivots clockwise as she grips knife arm at the wrist and pulls it forward past her body; she punches into face.

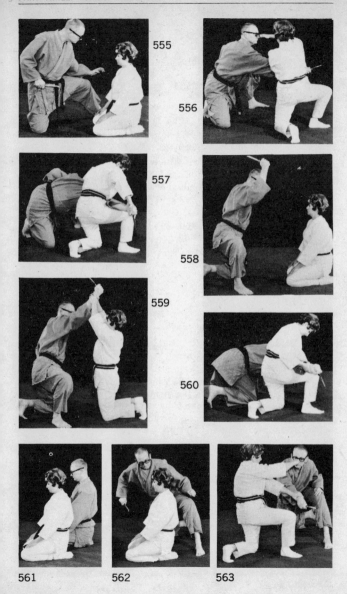

564

564.   Levering the captured arm over her bent leg, Defender
reaches around his neck with her left arm, gripping cloth at his
right lapel. Choke is applied (simulated) by pulling back with both
arms.

After hesitating a moment, both rise and return to starting kneeling
position. They hesitate in this position for a moment, then Attacker
walks to edge of mat, places dagger there and returns to stand in
front of Defender (about 12 feet apart); when Attacker stands
facing, Defender rises to stand.

TWO-HAND GRIP (ryote-dori)

565.   Taking steps in unison, Attacker and Defender face within
arm's reach.

566.   Attacker grips both wrists.

567.   Defender simulates kick into groin as she jerks both arms
outward wide, breaking his grip.

568, 569.   Defender grips Attacker's left wrist with her right
hand, turns counterclockwise and wheels his captured arm around
as she turns, pulling it under her right arm and locking it close to
her body. Pressure is simulated by pushing upward at his wrist
with both hands. They hesitate for a moment and then return to
starting standing position.

SHOULDER GRAB (sode-tori)

570.   From standing facing position, Attacker steps around to
left side of Defender; he hesitates a moment, then both take steps
in unison; as they walk, Attacker reaches for Defender's shoulder.

571.   Defender leans body away from Attacker and kicks into
his knee.

572.   Placing kicking foot down, Defender pivots counterclockwise and graps Attacker's right sleeve.

573.   Pivot is completed and Defender executes Kickback Throw.

When Attacker is on the mat, both hesitate, then return to standing facing position.

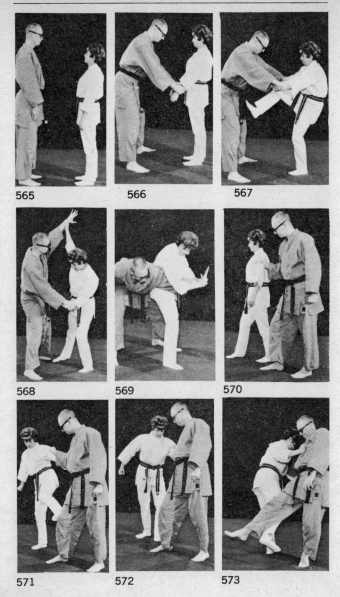

565

566

567

568

569

570

571

572

573

STRAIGHT PUNCH (tsuki-kake)

574.   From standing facing position, Attacker punches straight out; Defender sidesteps and parries punch with right hand.

575.   Defender takes another step behind Attacker and applies One-Arm Choke, with right arm around Attacker's throat and Defender's left hand gripping her right wrist. Pressure is simulated by pulling back. After a moment's hesitation, both return to standing facing position.

UPPERCUT (tsuki-agi)

576, 577.   From standing facing position, Attacker simulates uppercut fist blow; Defender grips moving arm at the wrist with both hands and pulls it upward.

578.   Maintaining her hold, Defender swings her body around clockwise and locks the captured arm under her left arm. Pressure is simulated by pushing upward.

After hesitating, both return to starting standing position.

HEEL-OF-PALM BLOW (suri-age)

579.   From starting standing position, Attacker simulates heel-of-palm blow.

580.   Defender parries blow with left hand as she delivers punch into midsection.

581.   Defender pivots in and applies left side Hip Throw.

When Attacker is on the mat, both hesitate, then return to starting standing position.

574

575

576

577

578

579

580

581

582   583   584

HAMMER BLOW (yoko-uchi)

582. From standing facing position, Attacker simulates hammer blow.

583. As Attacker hits, Defender steps forward under the striking arm and grips his left collar with her right hand(under his arm).

584. Defender takes another step behind him, into "T" position, and grips his right lapel with her left hand (under his arm). Pressure is simulated by scissor action.

585. This photo is a view of the same action as in photo 584 (taken from the rear).

After a moment of hesitation, both return to starting, standing position.

GROIN KICK (ke-age)

586. From standing facing position, Attacker simulates kick into groin.

587. As kicking foot moves forward, Defender sidesteps and hooks the leg with her left arm bent.

588. Defender grips captured ankle with both hands and counters with a groin kick.

After hesitating, both return to standing facing position.

STANDING BODY GRAB (ushiro-dori)

589, 590. From standing facing position, Attacker walks around behind Defender; he takes one step with his right foot and grips around upper body with his right arm; Defender grabs cloth of his arm with both hands.

591. Defender drops to right knee and pulls Attacker over her right shoulder.

585
586
587
588

589 590 591

592

592.   Defender simulates slashing blow into throat. Both hesitate for a moment and then return to standing facing position.

STANDING DAGGER THRUST (tsuki-komi)

593.   From facing standing position, Attacker walks to the edge of mat, takes dagger, returns to standing facing position, places dagger (in scabbard) inside his jacket. He draws dagger and simulates straight thrust forward.

594.   As knife hand moves toward her, Defender sidesteps clockwise, grips his wrist with her left hand and punches into his face.

595.   Defender continues clockwise turning, pulling the captured arm under her left arm and across her bent legs as she reaches around his neck with her left hand and grabs cloth at his right lapel. Pressure is simulated by pulling back with left hand and pulling up with right hand.

Photo 596 is the same action as photo 595 but from another angle. After hesitating, both return to standing facing position.

OVERHEAD DAGGER THRUST (kiri-komi)

597.   From standing facing position, Attacker simulates overhead dagger thrust.

598, 599.   As striking arm comes down, Defender grips wrist with both hands and wheels around clockwise, pulling the captured arm under her left arm and locking it into her body. Pressure is simulated by squatting down and levering the captured arm up.

They hesitate for a moment and then return to standing facing position.

SWORD DRAWING (nuki-kake)

From standing facing position, Attacker walks to edge of mat, replaces dagger and picks up sword; returns to facing position and slides sword into his belt.

Attacker makes gesture of drawing sword.

600.   Before sword is fully drawn, Defender steps in with right foot and grabs Attacker's right wrist with her right hand.

593

594

595

596

597

598

599

600

601   602

601, 602.   Defender steps behind Attacker, reaching over his arm
to grip right lapel with her left hand; Defender's right hand slides
under his right arm and is placed behind his head. Pressure is simulated. Both hesitate for a moment; return to starting standing position; Attacker places sword back into his belt.

STANDING OVERHEAD SWORD (kiri-oroshi)

603.   From starting position, Attacker draws the sword and holds
it (as shown) for an instant.

604, 605.   Attacker raises sword overhead and simulates downward slash; Defender sidesteps and grips his wrist with her right
hand.

606.   Turning clockwise, Defender wheels around, pulls captured
arm across her body as she puts her left arm around his neck,
gripping his right lapel. Pressure is simulated by pulling up with
the right hand and pulling back with the left hand.

Photo 607 is the same as photo 606, but from a different angle.

After hold is applied, Defender removes the sword; both hesitate,
then return to starting standing position. Defender holds sword
with both hands (palms up) and returns it to Attacker with formal
gesture (photo 608).

Attacker replaces sword in sheath; both take steps in unison backward until they are about 12 feet apart. Attacker then walks to
edge of mat and places sword there, returning to face Defender.
They then, in unison, reverse the procedure of beginning ceremonial bowing.

603

604

605

606

607

608

PART FOUR

SELF-DEFENSE AND SPORT FORMS—NEW STYLE

TIMES HAVE CHANGED!

There is nothing sacred about the forms of Judo. They were invented by Japanese humans and it should not be cause for shock than an American human has devised a new set of forms for modern practice. While the Old-Style forms are beautiful and quaint, we should remember that they were not intended to be quaint, they have become quaint with the passing of time. The forms of sword attack and forms of kneeling attack, for instance, were based on very ordinary situations of that time. The Japanese *did* carry swords and daggers; they *did* kneel instead of sitting on chairs. So, to invent forms which included these situations was a very natural development for that culture.

Moreover, the defense in the Old-Style forms was limited and determined by the culture in which they occurred. Grabbing and grappling with a dagger-wielding arm is not a good defense; from a kneeling position it might be the only possible defense. When performing the Old-Style forms, you should not be concerned with the practicality of the techniques, but only with performing them with style and grace.

I have now added some forms which are more appropriate to our time. Though you should not imagine that learning forms is the way of becoming completely proficient in street defense, at least, with these new forms, you are becoming familiar with movements and actions which have some resemblance to useful methods of street defense.

Students should be encouraged to invent additional forms. It is excellent, creative Judo practice to develop forms and demonstrate them. For the students who have no interest in contest and have completed the required Old-Style forms for degree advancement, the encouragement of personal creativity is a way of assuring their continuing interest in Judo. Formula learning develops only one part of the student; creativity develops a more interesting, lively, participating human being.

SELF-DEFENSE FORMS

Attack—Wrist Grip; Defense—Shoulder Throw
Attack—Fists; Defense—Hip Throw.
Attack—Fist; Defense—Back Straight Foot Throw
Attack—Shoulder Grab; Defense—Sweeping Foot Throw
Attack—Over-Arm Back Grab; Defense—Shoulder Throw
Attack—Back Choke; Defense—Kickback Throw
Attack—High Kick; Defense—Kickback Throw
Attack—Club; Defense—Reverse Hip Throw
Attack—Knife; Defense—Sweeping Foot Throw

WRIST GRIP; SHOULDER THROW

Both men stand in position of attention 12 feet apart; they bow to each other; both take steps simultaneously to come within arm's reach.

609. Attacker (left) grips both wrists of Defender.

610. Defender breaks wrist grip (refer to Basic Self-Defense, pp. 236, 237, for defenses).

611. After breaking wrist grip, Defender pivots in for One-Arm Over-Shoulder Throw.

612. Throw is executed.

613. Simulated stamping kick into armpit.

At the completion of the Form, Defender steps back into strong ready stance; then Attacker rises.

Both men return to starting position.

609   610   611

612

613

FIST ATTACK; HIP THROW

From starting position, both men step within arm's reach.

614, 615.   Attacker (left) simulates punching with one-two fist blows; Defender blocks blows.

616.   Defender pivots in for regular Hip Throw

After throw is completed, Defender steps back into strong ready stance; Attacker rises; both men return to starting position.

FIST ATTACK; BACK STRAIGHT FOOT THROW

Both men take steps to come within arm's reach.

617.   Attacker (left) punches with straight fist blow; Defender sidesteps and parries.

618.   Defender steps in for Reverse Straight Foot Throw.

After throw is executed, Defender steps back into strong ready stance; Attacker rises, both men return to starting position.

SHOULDER GRAB; SWEEPING FOOT THROW

From standard starting position, both men take a step to place them side by side, Attacker at left.

619.   Attacker grips Defender's shoulder.

620.   Defender applies Back Sweeping Foot Throw.

After throw is executed, Defender steps back into strong ready stance; Attacker rises; both men return to starting position.

OVER-ARM BACK GRAB; SHOULDER THROW

From standard starting position, men take simultaneous steps to place Attacker directly behind Defender.

621.   Attacker grips Defender's body around arms.

614   615   616

617

618

619   620   621

622   623   624

622.   Defender loosens grip of Attacker by taking deep breath, exhaling suddenly and dropping down as he forces outward with his elbows; then applies One-Arm Over-Shoulder Throw.

After executing throw, Defender steps back into strong ready stance; Attacker rises; both men return to starting position.

BACK CHOKE; KICKBACK THROW

From standard starting position, both men take simultaneous steps to place Attacker directly behind Defender.

623.   Attacker applies choke.

624, 625.   Defender loosens choking grip by jerking down on Attacker's arm; then turns body, prepares to apply Kickback Throw.

After throw is executed, Defender steps back into strong ready stance; Attacker rises; both men return to starting position.

HIGH KICK; KICKBACK THROW

From standard starting position, both men take a step back (within leg reach).

626.   Attacker (left) simulates kick into middle area, which Defender parries with forearm as he takes short step to the side.

627.   Defender applies Rear Sweeping Loin Throw.

After throw is executed, Defender steps back into strong ready position; Attacker rises; both men return to starting position.

CLUB; REVERSE HIP THROW

628.   From standard starting position, Attacker simulates overhead club attack; Defender steps forward and blocks the striking arm.

629.   Defender takes another step forward and applies Reverse Hip Throw.

After throw is completed, Defender assumes strong ready stance; Attacker rises; both men return to starting position.

625

626

627

628

629

KNIFE; SWEEPING FOOT THROW

From standard starting position, Attacker simulates straight-out knife thrust; Defender steps to side and kicks at Attacker's knee.

630, 631.   Defender then captures knife arm at wrist and elbow as he prepares to apply Sweeping Foot Throw.

After throw is applied, Defender steps into strong ready stance; Attacker rises; both men return to starting position; both men take one step back; bow.

SPORT FORMS

Over-Shoulder Throw and Side Shoulder Hold
Straight Foot Throw and Straight Arm Lock, Up
Sweeping Foot Throw and One-Arm Choke
Defense Against Standing Choke; Upper Innercut Throw
Combination Lifting Sweeping and Spring Foot Throws
Stiff-Arming and Counter Lifting Sweeping Foot Throw
Combination Sweeping Foot and Pull-down Straight Foot Throws
Circle Throw and Cross Arm Choke
Standing Choke and Innercut Throw
Leg Hip Throw and Cross Body Hold

The forms which I have devised differ from the Old-Style forms in two principal ways:

1. They are entirely Sport forms, whereas the Old-Style forms still include gestures and movements which indicate attack, rather than contest.

2. They combine various aspects of Judo in a more flexible manner, mixing throws, holds and chokes in a way which more nearly resembles combinations suitable for use in free-style exercise.

For the same reason that I encourage students to devise and invent new self-defense forms, I encourage students to invent new Sport forms—it is a splendid method of continuing, creative development.

632.   To begin this series of Sport forms, both players stand facing 12 feet apart (in the photo they are shown closer).

633.   They bow in unison.

634.   They take simultaneous steps to within arm's reach.

635.   They grasp each other in standard throwing fashion.

OVER-SHOULDER THROW AND SIDE SHOULDER HOLD

Starting from standard throwing position,

636.   Thrower pivots in for Over-Shoulder Throw.

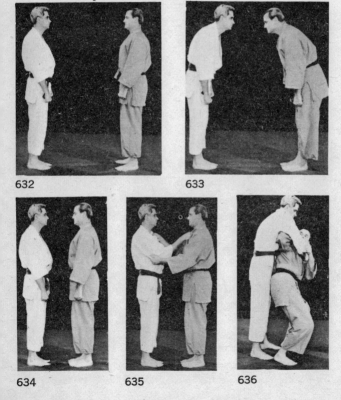

632

633

634

635

636

637. Throw is applied.

638. Thrower hesitates for a moment to show completion of throw.

639. Apply Side Shoulder Hold; maintain hold for the count of five to demonstrate proper techniques; both men rise and return to starting position.

STRAIGHT FOOT THROW AND STRAIGHT ARM LOCK

640. Thrower pivots in for Straight Foot Throw.

641. Apply throw.

642. When throw is completed, Thrower hesitates for a moment (to demonstrate good throwing technique).

643, 644. Thrower steps across Receiver with left leg and applies Arm Lock; hold is held for count of five; both men rise to starting position.

SWEEPING FOOT THROW AND ONE-ARM CHOKE

645.   From standard throwing position, Thrower tilts Receiver into position for Side Sweeping Foot Throw.

646.   Throw is applied; Thrower hesitates for a moment to show completion of throw.

641

642

643

644

645

646

647   648   649

647. Simulate application of One-Arm Choke; choke is held for count of five (without actual choking pressure) to demonstrate proper technique; both men rise to return to starting position.

DEFENSE AGAINST STANDING CHOKE; UPPER INNERCUT THROW

648. From standard throwing position, Receiver simulates standing Cross Arm Choke.

649. Thrower breaks choke as shown.

650, 651. Thrower then grips cloth at arms and applies Upper Innercut Throw; after completion of throw, with Receiver on the mat, both men hesitate for a moment; both men return to starting position.

COMBINATION LIFTING SWEEPING AND SPRING FOOT THROWS

652. From standard throwing position, Thrower simulates attempted Lifting Sweeping Foot Throw.

653. Thrower then pivots into position for Spring Foot Throw.

654. Throw is applied; with Receiver on the mat, both men hesitate for a moment before returning to starting position.

STIFF-ARMING AND COUNTER LIFTING SWEEPING FOOT THROW

655. From standard throwing starting position, Receiver stiff-arms Thrower.

656, 657. Thrower pulls Receiver forward, off balance, and applies Lifting Sweeping Foot Throw; with Receiver on the mat, both men hesitate for a moment before returning to starting position.

COMBINATION SWEEPING FOOT AND PULLING-DOWN STRAIGHT FOOT THROWS

658. From standard throwing position, Thrower simulates attempt at Sweeping Foot Throw.

650   651   652 ⟶

653   654   655 ⟍

656   657   658

H

659   660   661

662

663

659, 660.   Thrower drops into position for Pulling-down Straight Foot Throw and applies throw; with Receiver on the mat, both men hesitate for a moment before returning to starting position.

CIRCLE THROW AND CROSS ARM CHOKE

661, 662.   From standard starting throwing position, Thrower steps in and applies Circle Throw.

663.   When Receiver is thrown, Thrower rolls into backward somersault.

664.   Thrower straddles Receiver and simulates Cross Arm Choke; choking position is held for the count of five (without actual choking pressure) to demonstrate technique; both men rise to starting position.

STANDING CHOKE AND INNERCUT THROW

665.   From standard throwing starting position, Thrower simulates One-Arm Lapel Choke, which is intended as a feinting action.

666, 667. As Receiver responds to choking action, Thrower applies Innercut Throw; with Receiver on the mat, both men hesitate for a moment before returning to starting position.

LEG HIP THROW AND CROSS BODY HOLD

668. From standard throwing position, Thrower pivots in for Leg Hip Throw (this throw has not been shown before; it is a variation of Hip Throw—right leg of Thrower is bent and foot is placed in back of Receiver's foot).

669. Throw is executed.

664   665   666

667   668   669

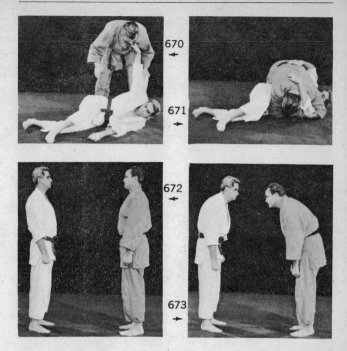

670. With Receiver on the mat, Thrower hesitates for a moment.

671. Thrower applies Cross Body Hold for the count of five; both men rise to starting position.

672. Both men take one step back.

673. They bow in unison.

PART FIVE

BASIC SELF-DEFENSE

INTRODUCTION

Students who are interested only in the sport of Judo are not required to study the work which follows. Do not make the mistake of thinking, however, that your sport training is practical for street defense. For the reasons discussed below, throwing *alone* is not useful as street defense for any except the very, very skilled Judoist. There are other techniques which require a great deal less training and are far more effective for modern street defense.

Techniques which have been selected for self-defense training here are basic. They are the most useful in the greatest number of actual situations; they are effective for smaller persons against larger assailants; they are not difficult to learn or remember; and will remain useful to you long after you are past your top physical form.

Some of the defenses are so simple that you have only to be familiar with them to put them to use if necessary; others require practice. The amount of time you devote to self-defense training depends on your interest. If you wish to gain considerable proficiency in techniques of self-defense, I recommend that you study from my *Complete Book of Self-Defense*.

For most people, neither sport Judo nor Aikido are effective methods of self-defense unless they are preceded by preliminary weakening actions such as the kicks of Ate-waza (or Karate, Savate or Yawara . . . the *kicks* are all similar, though there may be a difference in training methods and in combinations of kicks and hand blows). The kick shown here is common to many different kinds of unarmed fighting; it occurs in all the above named arts as well as in some others. It is not the *style* of kick which is important, it is its application for self-defense in a practical manner.

As an illustration of the uselessness of Sport Judo for self-defense, examine these photos.

674, 675. Obviously, this small woman cannot use fist fighting against a much larger opponent, for she comes into his fist range some inches before she is close enough to hit him.

674

675

676   677

676. In order to attempt a throwing action, she must move in even closer, placing herself in considerably more danger of a fist blow to her face. Those who advocate Judo throws for self-defense will say that the Judo thrower trains to become lightning fast and will throw before being hit. Nonsense. The very people who need self-defense training the most are those who cannot ever hope to become as nimble and swift as would be required for that.

677. How much easier and more practical to move out of fist range of an adversary and deliver a kick into his knee or shin.

HOW TO KICK: FIVE BEST FOOT BLOWS

678. The single most effective foot blow for practical street defense is with the bottom of the foot (or shoe). You should practice this kick so that you can deliver it with snap and force and without loss of balance. First, draw the knee up and then kick with the foot held as shown in the photo. This kick is useful because it does not require great precision to hit your target and because you can hit straight out, to the side, at midbody areas (as shown) or to the knee or shin.

679. With the edge of the foot (or shoe).

680. Stamping down with the bottom of the foot (or shoe).

681. Kicking straight forward with the ball of the foot. (When wearing shoes, kick with the toe.)

682. Stamping straight back with the bottom of the foot (or shoe).

HOW TO STRIKE: FIVE BEST HAND BLOWS

683. The single most effective hand blow is with the edge of the open hand. The point used for striking is the fleshy area between the wrist and the bone of the little finger. Cup the hand very slightly when hitting, and keep the thumb flat against forefinger.

678

679

680

681

682

683

You can strike with great force without hurting your hand if you strike properly. To determine the correct way of hitting, practice striking onto a table top or any hard surface. Begin with very light blows and increase the power a little at a time. If you strike incorrectly, you will feel pain at your wrist or little finger. Correct the angle until you can hit with force without feeling pain. This blow can be delivered with either hand, cross-body, in a downward direction, in an upward direction, palm up or palm down. It can be used to strike at bony surfaces, heavily muscled areas and into soft areas of the body.

684.   Extended Knuckle Blow: This blow is most effective when used into soft areas of the body. The extended knuckle concentrates the power of the blow.

685.   Extended Finger Blow: This jabbing, stabbing type of blow is only effective into soft parts of the body.

686.   Heel-of-the-Palm Blow: Though limited in the way it can be used, this is a very effective blow. Used for striking upward under the chin or nose, it can throw your assailant off balance and cause considerable pain.

687.   Elbow Blow: Especially useful as a backward blow, this puts all force of your arm and shoulder into it.

NERVE CENTERS AND PRESSURE POINTS

Instead of striking out wildly, you will greatly increase the effectiveness of your hand and foot blows if you learn some of the basic target areas—those vulnerable spots of the body which are known as nerve centers and pressure points. The ones I have selected are the most practical.

WHERE TO STRIKE—NONVIOLENT ATTACKS

The following target areas I classify as "safe" because they can be used to hurt or numb your adversary with very little possibility of serious or permanent injury. In the photos, man on right points to the target areas.

688.   Side of the neck, between ear and shoulder. An edge-of-the-hand blow (using either hand and using a backhanded palm down blow or a palm up blow) to this area is practical and effective. It can be hit from the rear or the front of your adversary; it is usually accessible and you can cause considerable pain with a moderate blow and even render him unconscious with a heavy blow.

689.   Solar plexus, just below where the ribs part, using an extended knuckle blow. A straight-in blow can knock the air out of your adversary; a blow delivered in an upward direction affects the heart, liver and lungs. Against a small person, a very powerful upward blow can be dangerous.

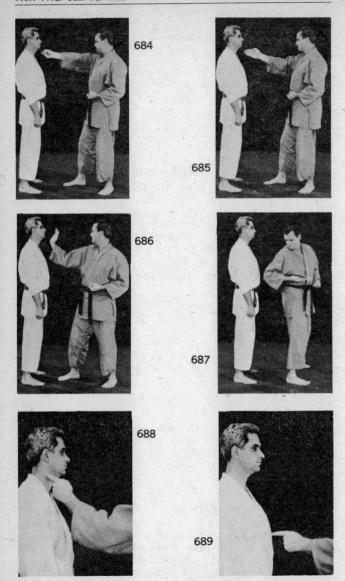

690. Elbow. If your adversary is in a boxing stance, you can strike into the bend of his elbow without coming within fist range.

691. Onto the high part of the forearm, about two inches below the elbow. If you stretch your arm forward, the higest part you see is the target area. A sharp blow to this spot has the same effect as hitting the "crazy bone"; a numbness and tingling result. A heavy blow can cause numbness from several minutes to half an hour, rendering his arm useless for that time.

WHERE TO STRIKE—LOW TARGET AREAS

692. Knee. Kicking into the knee is very effective for street defense. Even a slight person can kick with enough force to cause great pain to a larger, heavier assailant. Kicking at a 45° angle to the knee can cause dislocation.

693. Shin. One of the most sensitive areas of the body is the shin bone, where there is virtually no protective muscle or fat to shield it. Kicking at the shin and then scraping down the length of it with a shoe is extremely painful.

WHERE TO STRIKE—REAR TARGET AREAS

Side of the neck, as described earlier.

694. Kidney, or small of the back. A moderate hand blow can cause great pain; a heavy hand or foot blow can be dangerous.

695. Back of the knee. Excellent target for low kick; there is very little danger of serious or permanent injury but you can cause pain easily and even take your assailant down to the ground with a forceful kick into the back of the knee.

WHERE TO STRIKE—VIOLENT ATTACKS

If your adversary is making a violent attack, that is, he is trying to *injure or kill you*, you are justified in striking into the three areas described here. I classify them as "danger" areas, because there is the possibility of serious permanent injury or even fatality, if a heavy blow is struck into any one of these places. In no other instance are you justified in hitting into these target areas.

696. Temple. Slightly back from the corner of the eye, using edge-of-the-hand blow.

697. Into the eye, or eyes, using stabbing finger blow.

698. Directly onto the windpipe, using edge-of-the-hand blow or choke.

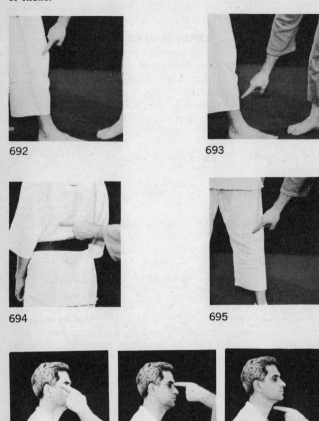

692   693

694   695

696   697   698

ANNOYING (Leaning, Grabbing, Bumping)

699.   Situation: Advisary might be leaning, grabbing or bumping you. The *precise* action is not important; the important thing, in this case, is that he is only being offensive, or annoying; he is *not* trying to harm or injure you.

Action: With an extended knuckle, dig into his side, just below the last rib. (There is a nerve center at that point.)

FRONT GRAB—ANNOYING AND SERIOUS

In the next three situations, there is a front grab of the body. The different responses to the three grabs are not due to the *type* of grab but are responses to the *intent* of the adversary.

700.   Situation: Front body grab, or reaching with intent to grab. No injury or harm is intended.

Action: With the heel of the palm, push or lightly hit up under the jaw.

701.   Situation: Front grab. Adversary is being more persistent than the adversary in photo 700 but does not intend serious harm or injury.

Action: Light poke into the hollow of the throat at the windpipe. A light blow into the windpipe is not dangerous, but it is very painful.

702.   Situation: Adversary is trying to harm or injure you.

Action: With the tips of the fingers, poke into the eyes. Only when you are being threatened with serious injury are you justified in using this defense.

WRIST GRAB DEFENSE—GRIPPING ONE HAND

703.   Your adversary has gripped one of your wrists with both hands. The grip, in itself, may not be a painful or harmful attack. It must be broken in order to avoid further aggressive action on his part and in order to free you to apply a throw, if required.

704, 705.   With your free hand, grab your captured hand. Utilizing muscle reaction, using jerky, quick motions, force forward until you feel the resisting upward pull, then jerk your hands up and free, cross-body. Follow with appropriate hand or foot blows, and throws, if required.

WRIST GRAB DEFENSE—GRIPPING BOTH WRISTS

706.   Your adversary has gripped both your wrists.

707, 708.   Muscle reaction is utilized for this escape, but it is a side to side movement. First, force your arms outward until you feel his resistance, then with quick, jerky motions, bring your arms inward and up. Your actual escape is from the opening between his thumb and fingers . . . the weakest part of his grip. Follow with hand and foot blows and throws, if required.

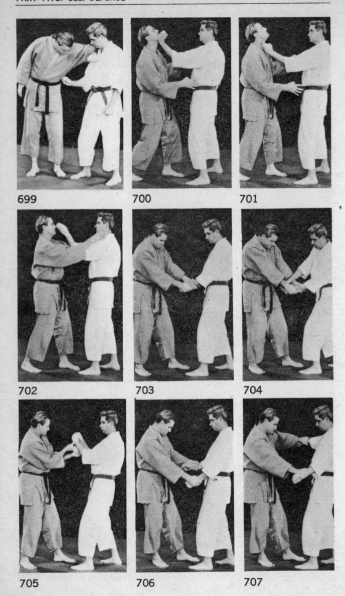

699

700

701

702

703

704

705

706

707

708   709   710

FRONT CHOKE DEFENSE NUMBER ONE

709. Situation: Your adversary has gripped your throat. The same action would be effective against a two-handed shoulder grab.

Action: With side of the hand blows, strike down with force onto the nerve centers of the forearms (about two inches below the elbow).

710. Follow with double hand blows into the sides of his neck. If necessary, continue to kick and strike. Apply throw, if required.

FRONT CHOKE DEFENSE NUMBER TWO

711. Situation: Same as for previous attack. The defenses are equally effective, it is a matter of personal choice which one you prefer. There is some possibility that you may find the first defense awkward to use if your adversary is considerably taller than you are. It is a good idea to know both these defenses.

Action: As adversary chokes (or attempts to choke) clasp your hands together (do not interlace you fingers) and 712 with a jerky, snappy action, drive your clasped hands up between his arms.

713. Follow with hand and foot blows and apply throw, if necessary.

FIST FIGHTING—CLOSE-IN

714. Using open-handed slashes, block *both* arms of your adversary. Even though he might only be punching with one arm, it is more effective to slash at both his arms.

715. After slashing, grip cloth (or arms) at his elbows and lock them out rigidly, as shown. You could not hold this position for very long, but just long enough to immobilize him while you

716, 717. kick him several times in the legs.

718. When he is hurt, turn him around and apply Straight Foot Throw, or rear takedown.

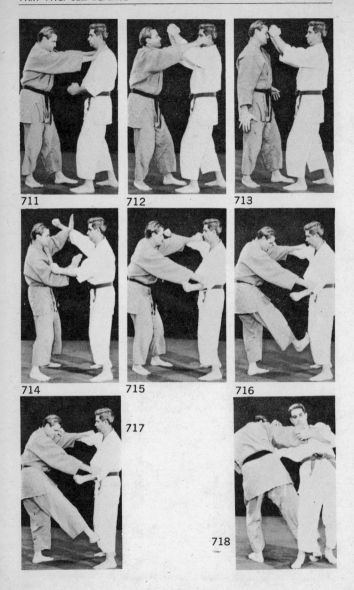

711

712

713

714

715

716

717

718

FIST FIGHTING—LONG RANGE NUMBER ONE

Although this defense is shown against a long-range punch (your adversary has to take one or more steps in order to get within fist range), it may also be used in other situations which are similar. The important determining factor is that your adversary is rushing you, and that he cannot hit you without moving in.

719. As adversary moves forward, take a step to the outside of his punching (or reaching) arm as you parry it with the palms of both hands. It is easier to *deflect* a rushing punch than it is to oppose it.

720. Kick into his leg.

Continue with other hand and foot blows, if necessary, and throw if required.

FIST FIGHTING—LONG RANGE NUMBER TWO

721. You are being threatened by an adversary who clearly intends to attack, but you are not within range of his fists. Do *not* move in close. From your safer position, kick into his knee or shin.

722. Immediately follow the first kick with a second.

723. Block both his arms (whether or not he actually attempts fist blows), but do not reverse the order of action; *kick first*.

724. Continue with several hand and foot blows until your adversary is visibly weakened.

725, 726. Spin him around and kick into the back of his knee.

If necessary, apply a rear throw to put him on the ground.

719

720

This is a complete defense against a violent unarmed attack. It is very likely that only part of the full defense will need to be used. It has been found, in actual use, that an adversary can be stopped with considerably less than the steps shown here. A defense should only be carried to the *necessary* point. You are neither justified nor permitted by law to continue past the point which is required by the situation.

FIST FIGHTING—LEAP KICK DEFENSE

727.   Getting out of fist range of your adversary is extremely important. When there is space to do so, at the first sign of aggressive action on the part of your adversary, leap out of range of his fist.

728.   From this safe range, kick into his leg and follow immediately with a second kick into his knee or shin.

If necessary, you can apply a throw after your adversary has been weakened in this manner.

THREATENED ATTACK

729.   This is a situation where you are being threatened by an adversary, but there is a possibility of avoiding a fight. You are prepared for your defense, even though your appearance and your stance are not belligerent.

730.   At the slightest sign of aggressive action on the part of your adversary (here he is shown making fists), thrust your hand into his face and yell. You are not trying to hit him but creating a distraction to startle and confuse him.

731.   Quickly kick into the knee or shin and follow it immediately with a second kick with your other foot.

After weakening your adversary in this manner, you can apply a throw, if necessary.

CLUB ATTACK—BACKHAND

The most common types of club (or stick) attack are the backhand overhead attack and the swinging attack from the side. The type of attack is clearly indicated by the preliminary movement of your opponent's hitting arm.

732.   As your adversary swings the club (or stick) forward to prepare to strike backhanded, with both your hands block his hitting arm.

727

728

729

730

731

732

733. Immediately grip cloth at his arm, locking it stiffly away from you and kick into his knee or shin.

If necessary, continue kicking, apply hold on his arm or throw.

For overhead blow, you can use the same defense, stepping sharply to the outside of the hitting arm to block it.

CLUB ATTACK—SIDE

734. As your adversary prepares to hit with a wide, swinging side blow, block his hitting arm with both your hands.

735. As you grip cloth at his sleeve with one hand, strike into the neck with your other hand and kick into the knee or shin.

Continue with hand and foot blows, as necessary. If needed, apply a backward tripping throw.

Please note: Sport Judo does not remotely prepare you to defend yourself against various back attacks. The movies and TV, to be sure, always have the hero prepared to hoist the villain over the shoulder at the slightest sign of back attack, but in films, the villian is paid to fall down. On the street, your adversary will not be so cooperative. In addition, unlike the movie villain who lets himself be thrown, the street villain is seriously trying to hurt or harm you.

BACK GRAB—UNDER ARMS

736. Your adversary has grabbed around the body. For training purpose, you can assume that there are two opponents and start your defense with a vigorous kick at the front opponent.

737, 738. Kick back into the shin or knee, and scrape down along the shin, stamping onto the instep.

739. Strike back into the thigh.

740, 741. Clasp your hands together (not interlacing your fingers) and swing your elbows around from side to side to hit into his face. As you strike, turn your head to look where you are striking.

The above sequence or techniques should be *more than enough* to effect release. If necessary, after release, turn to face your adversary and continue with hand and foot blows; finish with throw, if needed.

733   734 →   735

736   737   738

739   740   741

BACK GRAB—OVER ARMS

742. Adversary has gripped around the body, over your arms. Weaken your adversary with the same type of hand and foot blows as shown in Back Grab—Under Arms. Clasp your hands together (not interlacing your fingers) and take a deep breath to loosen his grip somewhat.

743. Exhale sharply and suddenly drop down. Exhaling should leave some room for you to drop down, as you have expanded his grip by inhaling.

744. Quickly follow this action with an elbow blow into his midsection. This action should effect release. If necessary, kick into the shin.

745. When release is effected, turn to face your adversary and kick into the knee. Continue with other hand and foot blows, if needed. Throw, if required.

BACK CHOKE

746. Adversary has applied a choke from the rear, using his arms to choke and pull you backward.

747. To relieve the pain, place one hand at his wrist and the other hand at his elbow and jerk down sharply. Turn your throat to the crook of his elbow.

748. Continue to jerk down on his arm as you kick into his shin.

749, 750. When the jerking down and repeated kicks into his legs have loosened his grip, lower yourself quickly and turn out from under his hold, maintaining your grip at his wrist.

751. Pull his arm around in back of him and kick into his knee as you pull up on his arm and pull him backward at the collar, taking him to the ground, if necessary.

745   746►

750 ↓   ↑ 747

748

↑ 749

751

752

HAIR GRAB

Though this defense is shown with a women, it is a fairly common back attack against men. The same defense can be used if you have been grabbed at the back of the collar.

752. Your adversary has grabbed from behind, and is pulling backward.

753

754

753. Put both your hands over the grabbing hand and press to your head. This action is to relieve the pain and to counter his backward pull.

754. Squat slightly, pivot on the ball of one foot and turn to face your adversary. Maintain your hold on his hand as you turn.

755. Kick into his knee or shin until he releases his grip. Continue with hand and foot blows as necessary; finish with throw, if needed.

SURPRISE BACK ATTACK

756. At sight (or sound or touch) which indicates a threat from the rear:*

757. Turn to *look at your adversary* as you slash up toward his head and take a step away. The step is to get out of hitting range and the blow is to parry his blow or, perhaps, to startle and distract him.

758. Kick into his knee or shin, and be prepared to follow with additional hand and foot blows, applying a throw if needed.

KNEE KICK DEFENSE

759. Your adversary starts to kick with the knee. Dodge to the outside of the kicking leg and:

760. Parry the kicking knee with open hand. Even though his leg is much stronger than your arm, you can *parry* the blow because you are merely deflecting the direction of the leg, not opposing it head on.

---

*You should learn to respond to threat of attack from the rear by training to react *before* the actual attack has been completed. You do not have to wait until a choke is applied, you should react at the slightest touch of hands at your throat or neck. You can learn to react at the sounds of steps behind you or even at the slightest sound of rustling or breathing. You can learn to react at the slightest sight of a hand reaching your peripheral vision.

755

756

757

758

759

760

761.   Parrying the blow will turn his body away from you. Move behind him, kick into the back of his knee. If necessary, you can take him to the ground by pulling back on his collar as you kick into the back of the knee.

Note: A toe kick can be done from close in or from just out of normal kicking range. A knee kick is done from close in.

TOE KICK DEFENSE

Because our legs are so much stronger than our arms, I suggest that the only practical defenses against kicking attacks are counterkicking or parrying. It is particularly difficult to attempt a throw if your adversary is kicking you. Trying to grapple with (or apply a hold onto) a kicking leg is impossible for any but the most highly trained people.

762.   Because your adversary signals his attack (by drawing his leg back to kick) you can learn to respond quickly and efficiently to the threat of kicking attacks. As your adversary prepares to kick, draw your leg up.

763.   As his leg comes forward, kick into his shin. Follow the first quick immediately with a second one.

764.   After you have hurt him, you may continue with several hand blows, if necessary, and finish with a throw, if required.

THREATENED KNIFE ATTACK

Unless you are in danger of *actual attack,* do not atempt a defense against a knife. If the knife is being used as a threat and the real intent is robbery, you would be wise to give up your money.

When the knife man intends to *use* his knife on you, you *must* make a defense as an alternative to simply standing still and allowing yourself to be sliced. Trying to throw a man holding a knife is utter folly. Even a champion Judo player would be taking a grave risk to move into knife range without first weakening and distracting the adversary.

765.   The knife man threatens attack, but is *not* moving in. There is no possibility of avoiding the attack, he seriously means to use his knife.

766.   Because he is not moving in, you take advantage of his stationary position to start your defense *before* he stabs. With a loud yell, thrust your hand in the direction of his eyes. You do not try to hit him with this action, but divert and startle him. If you have something you can throw (dirt, coins, a rock) do so.

761

762

763

764

765

766

767. Quickly follow the distraction action with a kick at the outside of his knife hand. This is not too high a kick if you have had any training at all, and kicking, rather than hand parrying, lets you hit him without putting your arms or body within knife range. Your legs are better protected (by trousers and shoes) than are your arms.

768, 769. Follow the first kick with another kick into his knee, then grip cloth at his upper arm and elbow and lock his knife hand away from you as you continue to kick him until he releases his grip on the knife. If necessary, at this point, you can apply a throw.

KNIFE ATTACK

770. The assailant is moving in to stab or slash.

771

772

773

771.   Leap to the outside of the knife hand and slash with back-hand blow at his forearm.

772.   Grip cloth at the arm, locking his arm rigidly away from you as you kick into his knee.

773.   Kick with the other foot, grip cloth at his upper arm or shoulder and continue to kick until he is visibly weakened and hurt. If necessary, at this point apply a throw.

GANG ATTACK NUMBER ONE

774.   A gang threatens attack, but they have not surrounded you.

775.   Do *not* wait for them to trap you in a circle. Leap to the outside edge of the group and kick with force at the knee of the closest man. (It is even more effective to hit the leader or largest man first, but do not place yourself in a vulnerable position to get him.)

776, 777.   After kicking him with force, grab him and shove him into the other men. (Do not maintain a hold on him, grip him only long enough to thrust him away.)

778, 781.   Kick and shove another man.

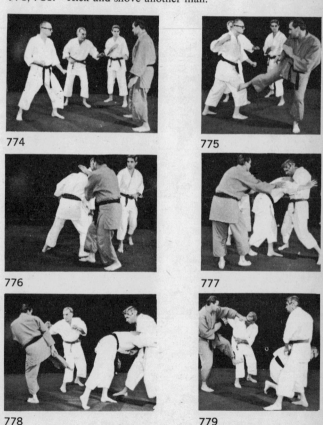

774

775

776

777

778

779

780

781

782

783

782–784.   Continue this action until you have taken the fight out of them, or visibly weakened them. A throw applied to one of the gang is very effective at this point.

GANG ATTACK NUMBER TWO

In defending against a gang attack you must immediately show that you will *not* be a willing and passive victim. Gangs are made up of individuals who are cowards . . . vicious cowards. There is no way to appeal to them for mercy; their sadistic pleasure is only increased at the sight of helplessness. Your only hope lies in taking the offensive when possible and concentrating on doing as much damage as you can as quickly as you can. If you can visibly hurt the largest person or the apparent leader of the gang, the others may not want to stand around and wait their turn to be hurt. Bullies and cowards only fight when they are certain of winning and they lose heart easily. If you cannot escape from a gang, you had better muster all the spirit you can and behave as though you are certain you can win.

784   785

786   787

785. When you are surrounded on all sides, your most effective defense is a series of multiple hand and foot blows, hitting more than one adversary each time. As an example, kick one man in front and slash back at a man to the rear.

786. Follow the first set of blows with a kick at the man to the rear and a slash to a man at the side.

787. Rotate, striking and kicking with force. Only when you see that someone is visibly weakened, should you attempt to throw. A throw at this point is especially useful; seeing one of their members on the ground is very discouraging to the other gang members.